Government
and Urban Poverty

Government
and Urban Poverty

Inside the policy-making process

Joan Higgins, Nicholas Deakin,
John Edwards and Malcolm Wicks

Basil Blackwell

First published 1983
Basil Blackwell Publisher Limited
108 Cowley Road, Oxford OX4 1JF, England

British Library Cataloguing in Publication Data

Government and urban poverty.
  1. City planning-Great Britain
  I. Higgins, Joan
  307.76'0941   HT169.G7
  ISBN 0-631-12937-5
  ISBN 0-631-13252-X Pbk

Typesetting by Oxford Publishing Services, Oxford
Printed in Great Britain by Billing and Sons Limited, Worcester.

Contents

Preface

A number of books in recent years have examined the problems of the inner cities and of urban deprivation and urban crisis. The present work attempts to add a new dimension to that literature by providing a detailed account of the policy-making process from the 'inside'. Three of the four authors were, at different times and in different ways, 'insiders' in the process and, from their experience in central and local government, can offer an important perspective. Nicholas Deakin was a civil servant, an independent researcher and, subsequently, head of the GLC Central Policy Unit. John Edwards worked in the Home Office on an evaluation of the Urban Programme, and Malcolm Wicks was Social Policy Analyst in the Urban Deprivation Unit of the Home Office.

The book has been very much a cooperative enterprise. It is the result of a series of meetings and a number of drafts, which have been commented upon by each of the authors. Joan Higgins wrote chapters 1 and 2 and had overall editorial responsibility; John Edwards wrote chapter 3, Malcolm Wicks chapter 4 and Nicholas Deakin chapter 5. Each of the authors wrote sections of the concluding chapter, and Joan Higgins edited the final version.

1

Introduction

The conclusions of the Rt. Hon. the Lord Scarman, in his
report on the Brixton riots of April 1981, suggest that thinking
on urban policy in Britain, in a little over a decade, has come
full circle. He ends with the words of President Lyndon
Johnson in his address to the US National Advisory Commission on Civil Disorders in 1968:

> The only genuine, long-range solution for what has hap-
> pened lies in an attack – mounted at every level – upon
> the conditions that breed despair and violence. All of us
> know what those conditions are: ignorance, discrimi-
> nation, slums, poverty, disease, not enough jobs. We
> should attack these conditions – not because we are
> frightened by conflict, but because we are fired by con-
> science. We should attack them because there is simply
> no other way to achieve a decent and orderly society in
> America.

'These words', Lord Scarman concluded, 'are as true of Britain today as they have been proved by subsequent events to
be true of America' (Scarman Report, 1981 p. 136).

If America knew in 1968 what the problems of its inner
cities were, so too did Britain when the first of the initiatives
described in this book began. The evidence of innumerable
research reports some 14 years later serves simply to underline
the accuracy of the analysis. For the most part, the only

change that has taken place has been in the lives of the
residents of run-down, decaying areas of the cities, where their
problems of poverty have deepened and where jobs have been
in even shorter supply. The many and varied attempts,
described in these pages, to change the direction of social
policies in ways that would benefit the urban poor have been
singularly unsuccessful. But there has been no shortage of
good will, no shortage of imaginative ideas for regenerating
depressed areas, no shortage of research and experimentation,
and no shortage of volunteers willing and eager to seek a
solution. Why, then, are the problems of urban poverty today
as bad as, if not worse than, they were in the late 1960s, when
many of the 'urban experiments' began? Why have we failed
to learn the lessons spelled out in the literature emanating
from our various inquiries?

This book sets out to find some of the answers to these
questions. It is concerned with two issues in particular: first,
with the role of central government in the making and
implementation of policies for the inner cities, and, second,
with the ways in which knowledge for policy can be accumulated or lost in the labyrinth of experimentation and research.
At first glance, it seems that it is not a lack of knowledge about
urban problems, and policies to resolve them, that accounts
for the relative lack of success of the programmes described
here. There were more than 200 reports, of various kinds,
from the Community Development Project alone, a thorough
and detailed analysis of the Urban Programme (see Edwards
and Batley, 1978), specially commissioned research on the
Comprehensive Community Programme and Inner Area
Studies, and a number of evaluations of inner-city policy after
1977 (including the establishment of an Inner Cities Working
Party by the SSRC). But this accumulated knowledge, in itself,
did nothing to arrest the outbreaks of violence and rioting that
took place in many of the major cities of Britain in 1981. The
mere existence of knowledge does not change policy or
improve social conditions.

Tied in with the issue of knowledge and policy is that of
experimentation. To greater and lesser degrees, each of the
initiatives described here was intended to be experimental,

though in none of them was it clear what the nature of the experiment would be or how the results would be fed back into the policy-making process. Obviously, there are varying standards of rigidity in experimentation, ranging from projects that are experimental in the sense of incorporating new and untried methods, to those that are carefully formulated in terms of clear-cut objectives and are strictly monitored. There was little evidence of the latter approach in these programmes. Indeed, critics have argued that successive governments were not interested in any new knowledge that the programmes might produce, but found it convenient to describe them as 'experiments' because this justified low levels of activity, in just a few areas of the country, at relatively little cost.

A book such as this must ask whether the experiments failed to make lessons for policy sufficiently explicit; whether the essential elements of a solution were buried so deep in the literature and rhetoric of urban reform that they did not make an impact. Was it simply a failure of communication? Or was it, on the other hand, a resistance on the part of policy-makers and politicians to learning the lessons of past experience? None of the solutions envisaged was cost-free, and the majority implied the commitment of resources on a vast scale if any real progress was to be made. The economic climate in the late 1960s and early 1970s was (as now) scarcely favourable for ambitious and expensive programmes of social reform. The chapters that follow illustrate, however, that without such a commitment and an attack – as President Johnson suggested 'mounted at every level . . . upon the conditions that breed despair and violence' – the items on the agenda will be exactly the same in the next decade, when 'the urban problem' raises its head again.

CHRONOLOGY

One obvious question is whether, and how, the programmes described here are linked together. Was each programme a more refined and sophisticated version of that which preceded it? How similar were their aims and conceptions of the problem, and to what extent did they build upon what had gone before? While in some respects these programmes bore superficial similarities, in others they differed quite significantly. The Community Development Programme, for example, began with a concern for 'communities' and with delinquency, and was not designed as a poverty programme at all. The Urban Programme, according to John Edwards, was not a social programme, but rather 'a money-spending mechanism' (and one concerned particularly with racial disadvantage), while the policies described by Nicholas Deakin focus specifically on the needs of the inner city. This section gives a brief account of how these various approaches evolved and the points at which they impinged upon each other.

The Urban Programme was the first of the urban initiatives to become established. It was announced by Harold Wilson, then Prime Minister, on 5 May 1968, amidst growing concern about 'multiple deprivation', urban poverty and race relations. According to James Callaghan, Home Secretary, whose Department was to take control of the Programme, it was designed to deal with the 'relatively small pockets of severe social deprivation' in the cities and towns of Britain. His expectations of the Programme were that it would 'supplement the government's other social and legislative measures to ensure, as far as we can, that all our citizens have an equal opportunity in life' (Hansard, vol.769, 22 July 1968).

Hard on the heels of the Urban Programme (UP), in July 1969, came the formal announcement of the Community Development Project (CDP). However despite, its similar aims and emphases, it did not in any sense arise out of the earlier programme. It was the result of discussions that, to a large extent, parallelled – and only occasionally overlapped – those surrounding the establishment of the UP. Indeed, although some of the same personnel were involved with both initiatives within the Home Office, those concerned particularly with the CDP were anxious that the premature and hasty announcement of the UP might undermine support for the proposals on which they had been working. According to Edwards and Batley, Home Office officials who had been drawing up plans for the CDP were 'taken aback and were left wondering whether their ideas had come to fruition or had been pre-empted' (Edwards and Batley, 1978, p. 41). In the event, the fates of the two programmes – at least administratively – became joined. The CDP was financed out of earmarked UP funds, and in 1970, when the Children's Department (which had been responsible for the CDP) moved from the Home Office, both programmes were run by the new Community Programmes Department. In some ways the alliance between the CDP and the UP was a marriage of convenience, and the ties that bound became weakened when the CDP fell into disfavour some years later. Although the CDP had followed on, chronologically, from the UP, it represented not so much the outcome of a refinement of ideas or a narrowing down of objectives as a separate development of similar concepts and policies. This is important when we draw conclusions about the growth and sharing of knowledge within and between the programmes discussed here.

The next major initiative to come from the Home Office was the launch, in July 1974, of 'a new strategy for tackling urban deprivation' and the setting up of the Comprehensive Community Programme (CCP). By 1974 it seemed that the problems of the cities were now defined in a somewhat different way from that which had been the case five years earlier. There was a new emphasis on better coordination of services, on the improvement of management structures, and on efficiency rather than upon 'individual, family and community malfunctioning' (CDP), or upon the increase of resources for inner-city areas. In the view of some writers the CCP, in this respect, signified the learning of lessons from previous programmes and an advance in thinking at the policy level. Lawless has argued, for example, that they were both 'a reflection and a development of official thinking about urban deprivation' (Lawless, 1979, p. 89). As Malcolm Wicks in chapter 4 explains, the CCP was intended to undertake brief analyses of the problems of six areas rather than embarking upon lengthy research programmes, and was to evaluate the effects of existing policies. It was expected that it would devise comprehensive programmes of action that would bring together many local agencies, including water and health authorities, voluntary bodies and residents, to determine priorities for future action.

In the meantime, the Department of the Environment (DOE)

had also initiated a series of research projects on urban deprivation, given a boost by Peter Walker's announcement of a new
'total approach' to the cities, in July 1972. The best known of
these were probably the Inner Area Studies (IAS), which – like
the CCP that came later – laid emphasis upon a coordinated
attack on the problems of inner cities. The Inner Area Studies
established in Birmingham, Liverpool and Lambeth are
important to the story told here for perhaps two reasons. First,
they were instrumental in shifting the focus away from individual pathology as a prime cause of urban deprivation and in
beginning to look instead at the problems of 'powers,
resources and techniques'. Second, they formed a test-bed for
theories that were later to inform the inner-area policies
described by Nicholas Deakin in chapter 5.

If we were looking for a mechanism for tying together the
various strands of policy and practice evolved in the urban
initiatives from 1968 onwards, the 1977 White Paper, '*Policy
for the Inner Cities*' (DOE, 1977e), seemed to be it. In the
opening paragraph it claimed to have drawn upon 'the
experience of earlier initiatives, including the Urban
Programme', and to owe 'a great deal to the studies and
experiments of recent years: the Educational Priority Areas,
Community Development Project, Area Management trials,
development work on the Comprehensive Community
Programme, the studies of the London docklands and above
all the three Inner Area Studies' (para. 1, p. 1). Certainly the
White Paper underlined the importance of structural factors in
the decline of the inner cities – pointing particularly to 'economic decline' and the structure of the labour market, 'physical
decay', 'social disadvantage' and the added problems
experienced by 'ethnic minorities'. The solutions envisaged in
the White Paper were, in Peter Shore's view, 'the first comprehensive policy for the inner cities which this country has
ever had'. Nicholas Deakin's chapter evaluates the actual
impact of this attempt to draw together the different strands of
reform in the inner cities.

All of these proposals, however, tended to beg the question
of whether there was actually an 'inner cities problem'. What
they showed was that there was a constellation of forces

involving jobs, housing, race and inequality, which, in a number of urban areas, manifest themselves in terms of squalor, deprivation and decay. However, as a number of writers have suggested, these features were not peculiar to the cities and were increasingly evident in many areas across the country. A specific focus upon a select number of towns and cities – Birmingham, Liverpool, London – created the impression that poverty was just an isolated occurrence and could be overcome with the injection of relatively small sums of money. But the critics were not slow to point out that there were far more people living in deprived circumstances outside the 'pockets of poverty' than there were within them.

Nevertheless, despite these reservations, this relatively short period (in policy terms) of 14 years or so did see an important shift in the perception of the causes of social deprivation. The period began with Derek Morell's analysis of social problems (in his plans for community development areas) in terms of 'individual, family and community malfunctioning', and ended with Lord Scarman's conclusions about the 'structural cause of unemployment', the 'lack of an effective coordinated approach to tackling inner-city problems' and 'acute housing stress'. The emphasis had shifted from blaming the individual or the community to looking at economic factors at the national level, and at the inadequacies of the social policies of both central and local government. No such advance in thinking is irreversible, of course, and it will not be consistent across different policy areas or among different interest groups. This is illustrated by the fact that some observers of the 1981 riots attributed them to lack of employment prospects for the young, especially black males, while others sought explanations in terms of 'bad parenting' or other behavioural factors. Similarly, while structural causes may be seen as of relevance in inner-city problems, failings of the individual may still be held to be responsible for unemployment and poverty. In the chapters that follow the authors have paid particular attention to the question of how the problems were defined and conceptualized in each of the programmes described here.

CONTEXT

The context in which these programmes evolved was not one that was conducive to major programmes of social reform. From the late 1960s onwards a primary aim of successive governments – Labour and Conservative alike – had been to contain, if not reduce, public expenditure. The prospect of new, big-spending social programmes was, to say the least, remote, and any new policy initiative had to develop within these constraints. This partly explains why those programmes that did emerge tended to take the form of small-scale, inexpensive 'experiments' like the CDP or programmes offering new ways of delivering the goods more cost-effectively. Both John Edwards and Nicholas Deakin, for example, in their chapters describe the programmes covered as essentially administrative reforms. 'The determining factors of the structure and process of the Urban Programme', for instance, were said to be 'largely administrative convenience and feasibility', while the White Paper on policy for the inner cities represented 'the search for the most effective administrative solution' (pp. E73, 118). The late 1960s and early 1970s were a period of some upheaval in the health and social services, with the reorganization of the personal social services, local government and the National Health Service. The policy themes of the period were 'coordination', 'rationalization' and 'efficiency'. The recommendations of the Central Policy Review Staff for a 'joint approach to social policy' became, at least in theory, a guiding principle. The innovative tones of the 1960s had given way to the cautious managerialism of the 1970s.

The period also saw the beginnings of what has been described as the 'welfare backlash'. This manifests itself in an apparent electoral unpopularity of social welfare measures, but more particularly in an unwillingness among certain sectors of the population to pay taxes that contribute to the funding of health and welfare services. This growing antipathy to public welfare has been evident not only in the United Kingdom but in other European countries, Australia and the United States. It has been exacerbated by broader economic crises of varying proportions, resulting in inflation, high unemployment and rising prices. The pattern of policy response, reflected in programmes for the urban poor and the inner cities, follows that established in the United States particularly in the second half of the 1960s. As most of the authors have pointed out, the influence of American ideas was an important factor in the early days of the British programmes. For the most part, however, as has been suggested elsewhere (Deakin, 1974, Higgins, 1980), the lessons learned from America were the wrong ones, or they were misunderstood or misinterpreted. In any event, the assumption that American perspectives could simply be transplanted, unmodified, to the British situation soon met with difficulties.

It was partly as a result of American influences that the concept of an 'inner-city problem' became fashionable. In the late 1960s it was barely an issue at all (or it appeared under different guises); by the late 1970s it was one of *the* major issues for policy-makers. However, comparisons with America were misleading. The causes of inner-city blight in the United States differed in significant respects (associated especially with the financing of urban services) from those in Britain. Although some of the fundamental economic factors involved remained the same, as the new breed of urban sociologists (Castells, O'Connor and others) were pointing out, the manifestations were different and required different solutions. The notion of an 'inner-city problem' was an attractive one to policy-makers, however. It meant that problems could be isolated and were potentially containable within identified geographical areas. From Galbraith's concept of 'insular poverty' in the late 1950s, then, we had moved through Keith Joseph's 'pockets of poverty' to 'black spots', 'needlepoints' and 'black holes'. In all this, as John Edwards points out, what had changed was not so much the nature of the problem as our social construction of it. The contributors to the book are, to a degree, sceptical about the presentation of the 'inner-city problem' and about the apparent tendency to redefine the problem to fit the available, or desired, solutions.

Associated with the social construction of social problems as being spatial in their origin and effects was the growth of area-based policies to deal with them. However, as Malcolm

Wicks has argued elsewhere (Wicks, 1978), there has been no clear understanding of how the emphasis on area deprivation arose and what particular issues it was meant to confront. He argues that the area approach not only suited the economic constraints of the time, but also met some of the growing anxieties about changes in politics and administration. Problems were seen in the widening gap between the individual and the state, the access of citizens to the decision-making process and the accountability of elected officials. The alienation of citizens from government was thought to be accompanied by a decline in 'community' – a shift away from social units that provided for all the needs of their members without recourse to outside intervention. The renewed interest in small-area projects was, in part, seen as a response to these trends. It was an attempt to counteract the ever-increasing size of units of administration and institutions. It may also have been seen as a way of improving efficiency and achieving greater cost-effectiveness and more efficient management. Selectivity in provision, it was assumed, meant services and benefits going to those who most needed them rather than having them thinly spread across many groups and areas. Finally, and importantly, Wicks argues, the area approach was closely tied in to the question of race. If ethnic minorities were geographically concentrated, area-based policies seemed an appropriate way of reaching immigrant groups. As we shall see in later chapters, some of these assumptions proved to be either misconceived or unjustified, but the point remains that different groups saw, in the area approach, the solutions to different problems, and there was no unanimity about what was being advocated and why.

In this book we hope from the detailed analysis of a 14-year period of policy-making to make some contribution to an understanding of how social policies are made and implemented. The case studies illustrate the importance of particular determinants of policy – civil service values and perspectives, administrative issues, political expediency and economic constraints among others. To this extent they are a test of different theories of policy-making in the literature of political science and social policy that have developed in the last decade. The exercise is an important one, for very pragmatic reasons. The conditions that gave rise to violence and protest in Notting Hill in the 1950s, in Watts, Chicago and Detroit in the 1960s, in a whole series of incidents in the 1970s and 1980s, culminating in riots in St Paul's, Brixton, Toxteth and Moss Side, remain virtually unchanged. Indeed, many would argue that discrimination, inequality and poverty have grown worse in the last 30 years. The fuse to the powder keg of urban violence grows shorter all the time, and unless the lessons emerging from these pages are learned by policy-makers and politicians alike, further, and bigger, explosions are inevitable.

2

The Community Development Project

The Community Development Project was the second, but perhaps the most controversial, of a series of projects in the late 1960s and 1970s concerned with urban deprivation. It was an ambitious programme in scope, but modest in terms of expenditure costing only some £5 million over eight or nine years. This chapter charts the early development of the Project and examines the influences that shaped its subsequent progress.

When the Project was fully operational, it consisted of 12 action and research teams in different parts of the country, run from the Home Office by a central research team. The organization at the central level, however, changed in a number of ways between 1969, when it effectively began, and 1978, when – in most respects – it had come to an end. These changes are described in greater detail below. At the local level, it was intended that the action teams would be supported by a research team from a 'nearby university'. The aim was never fully realized, but arrangements for monitoring and evaluation were eventually established. The local authorities hosting projects, with the name of the projects areas and the institutions responsible for research, were as follows:

Coventry (Hillfields); INLOGOV, Birmingham University
Liverpool (Vauxhall); Social Evaluation Unit, Oxford
 University

Southwark (Newington); South Bank Polytechnic
Newham (Canning Town); Centre for Institutional
Studies, North East London Polytechnic
West Riding (Batley); Department of Social
Administration, University of York
Paisley (Ferguslie Park); Department of Social and
Economic Research, Glasgow University
Newcastle (Benwell); Department of Sociology and Social
Administration, University of Durham
Cumberland (Cleator Moor); Department of Social
Administration, University of York.
Birmingham (Saltley); Social Evaluation Unit, Oxford
University
Tynemouth (Percy and Trinity); Department of
Behavioural Studies, Newcastle Polytechnic
Oldham (Clarksfield); Department of Social
Administration, University of York

The project areas varied in size from populations of 42,400
(Canning Town) to 8,600 (Glyncorrwg), although the norm
was approximately 15,000. With the exception of Cleator
Moor and Glyncorrwg, they were located in urban areas
displaying many aspects of 'multiple deprivation'. These factors included lower than average incomes, higher than average
unemployment rates, high dependence on state benefits, poor
standards of health (especially high infant mortality rates),
poor housing, lack of basic amenities and general environmental squalor. Most of them had also suffered serious economic
and industrial decline and loss of population.

Much has been written about the origins of the Community
Development Project (CDP) and about the motives of policy-
makers in central government in establishing it in the way it
did, when it did. These accounts range from those emphasizing its 'social control' elements (Bridges, 1975; Cockburn,
1978; Corkey and Craig, 1978) to those who see it as part of
the overall attempt, in the late 1960s, to reorganize health
services, personal social services and education in ways that
would make them more responsive to local needs and allow
'consumers' a greater degree of involvement in their planning
(Mayo, 1975). The following section discusses factors that

may have had a bearing upon the decision to launch the Project. It also examines the extent to which the theories of the origins of the CDP measure up to the available evidence on its genesis.

ORIGINS

There is little doubt that the original initiative in developing the Project came from within the civil service – indeed, from within the Home Office and from one civil servant in particular: Derek Morrell. In 1969 Morrell was Assistant Under Secretary in charge of the Children's Department in the Home Office – what was to be the culmination of a varied and illustrious career. After Oxford and war service, he had joined the Ministry of Education in 1947. He first made his mark in the Architects and Buildings branch, and was instrumental in setting up the Architects' Development Group. He was Private Secretary to three Ministers of Education and moved on to one of his most notable successes, the establishment of the Curriculum Studies Group and subsequently the Schools Council (of which he became Secretary). He was an enthusiastic and energetic advocate of curriculum development and reform. In 1966 he moved to the Home Office where, as John Banks put it, his 'considerable power in getting things done' resulted in the 1969 Children and Young Persons Act and the Community Development Project. Because of their profound influence on the original conception of the CDP, it is worth examining Morrell's values and beliefs a little further.

The idea of promoting a coherent strategy of community development was originally discussed by civil servants in the Home Office in the course of devising proposals for changes in the law relating to children and young persons. In Morrell's eyes, the new initiative was an attempt to deal with some of the unresolved problems that lay beyond the scope of the White Paper, *Children in Trouble*, and to broaden the notion of community development from the hitherto narrow interest in children and young offenders. A decision was taken, at the end of 1967, to set up an inter-departmental working party to develop these ideas. It met for the first time on 17 January 1968 and had representatives from eight major government departments. A good deal was accomplished in that first meeting, under the chairmanship of Morrell. They discussed the possible size and choice of areas for an experiment in community development, including the kind of social indicators that could be used in selecting areas. They raised issues about the notion of positive discrimination and heard about the various similar experiments in community development that were already under way in the United States. Finally, they emphasized the need to work towards the coordination of existing social services. In further meetings, on 19 February, 2 April and 20 May 1968, these and other issues – such as the need for evaluation and monitoring – were discussed in more detail, and by June 1968 the Working Party was able to present a set of firm proposals in a document drafted by Morrell.

In the Report of the Inter-departmental Working Party, entitled *Community Development – An Experiment in Social Growth*, which appeared on 21 June, Morrell set out the likely cost and administration of the proposed scheme. The Working Party envisaged an annual budget of £90,000 for the 'action' component (12 community development teams employing 36 people) and at least £60,000 for the research. Ideas about the organization and structure of the local teams were also included. The Report emphasized the need to coordinate the scheme's activities with those responsible for the proposed reorganization of the personal social services, then under discussion by the Seebohm Committee. It also suggested the establishment of a central steering committee for the project, based in Whitehall, to oversee developments across a number of government departments.

Perhaps the most interesting aspects of the Working Party Report were the insights it offered into Morrell's own philosophy of social reform and his expectations of what, at that stage, he described as 'community development areas'. It is significant that he referred to the scheme as an 'experiment in social growth'. The project was not conceived as a poverty programme in any but the broadest sense, and its main thrust was towards encouraging the personal and moral growth of individuals, and the growth of hope and enthusiasm in declining communities. Morrell saw the exercise essentially as one of 'pump-priming'. Relatively small sums of government money would be directed to a number of communities that might be expected to make imaginative use of them.

As John Banks explains, Morrell's civil service career had been dominated by his view of the 'totality of human experience', and it is this that shone clearly through his ideas about community development. It was a powerful and pervasive philosophy, and one strongly influenced by his commitment to Christianity and to Catholicism. Banks continues:

> The growth of whole persons in community through the formation of creative relationships – this was the theme for the family, the school and society at large. To enlarge the opportunities for such relationships was the task he discovered for himself. In it his personal vision of the Christian ethic and his view of the role of government in social policy were fused. [*Times Educational Supplement*, 19 December 1969]

In aiming to achieve these ends, Morrell had a strong commitment both to cooperative effort and to 'rationality'. It has been said of him that 'with his own remarkable gift of enlisting cooperation, he was at his happiest and most effective when furthering proposals for bringing people and services together' (*The Times*, 19 December 1969), and that 'much of his writing and public speaking was aimed at defining the requirements for cooperative social action' (*Times Educational Supplement*, 19 December 1969). His commitment to rationality was evident in a number of spheres, not least in his conception of the role of evaluation in the CDP. He believed firmly that social experiments could be conducted that would test out hypotheses and produce plausible results. At the Ditchley Conference, held in October 1969 to discuss various aspects of the Community Development Project, Morrell explained that as he saw it, 'what the conference stood for was the increasing use of scientific method in decision-taking. . . . The sequence of scientific inquiry should be kept in mind: first action, then observation, then the formation of hypotheses, and then their testing' (Home Office, 1969).

On 9 July 1968, Morrell's Report was put before the Social Services Committee. As Richard Crossman explains, it was 'a quite unprecedented paper from the Home Office'. It was, he goes on, 'nothing like the normal Civil Service brief outlining a new idea, but a philosophical paper on a project developed by a man called Derek Morrell'. Crossman's assessment of Morrell was an interesting one that corresponds with that of most of the latter's acquaintances. He had been, he said, 'an enormously important and dynamic factor at Education', who, since his transfer to the Home Office, 'had been fighting the battle to make the Home Office the central pivotal office of social welfare. He is by no means a normal civil servant,' Crossman continued. 'He's a red-faced, explosive man with an enormously inflated public-school sense of morality and it's he who put Jim Callaghan up to this proposal which breaks every law and precedent' (Crossman, 1977, p. 125).

During the first half of 1968, then, there had been fruitful and positive cooperation between civil servants in at least eight government Departments, resulting in detailed proposals for community development areas which came through the 9 July meeting almost unchallenged. The suggestion in some circles, therefore, that Harold Wilson himself had dreamed up the idea of the CDP, as a response to Enoch Powell's 'rivers of blood' speech (made in April 1968), seems completely without foundation. While the Urban Programme, as a whole, may have been – as G. Smith and T. Smith described it – 'hastily assembled as a result of Powell' (*New Society*, 30 December 1971), this could not have been said of that component of it that became the CDP.

The Inter-departmental Working Party had met three times before Powell's speech on 20 April, and carefully researched and costed proposals for the Project were already well advanced. That is not to say that the Powell speech did not create a political climate in which the prospects for new initiatives on 'community', 'race' and 'urban deprivation' were especially favourable. Indeed, the civil servants involved in drafting the proposals were probably as surprised as anyone by the speed with which the scheme won approval. This is no doubt due partially to the fact that Morrell had canvassed, and won over, most of the crucial decision-makers, but it was also clear that the Government urgently needed to be seen to be taking action on the problems of the cities. However, while the scheme won acceptance from the Government, it provoked little or no interest in the Parliamentary Labour Party, except in so far as it had potential as a cosmetic exercise. There were few Parliamentary discussions of the Project, and politicians generally seemed to be suspicious of it. Richard Crossman was mildly enthusiastic, but only if he (as Secretary of State for Social Services) could have control over it. James Callaghan, who originally supported Morrell appears later to have had a change of heart. Richard Crossman's account of a meeting of the Social Services Committee on 16 July 1968 describes how this volte-face occurred:

> At Social Services Committee we had another discussion of this extraordinary community experiment idea the Home Office has put forward, drafted by Derek Morrell. He made a curiously Buchmanite kind of religious speech about action changing lives and I suddenly heard him saying, 'There must be a second revolution in the welfare state, a second revolution.' I was more amazed than ever that the official paper had been accepted without a word of criticism from any other Department, though it's an astonishing mix-up of sociology and mystical religion. Then came a very dramatic moment. Jim suddenly said, 'We must stop all this bloody religious nonsense.' Had the Home Office put this idea forward without taking him into their confidence? No, I fancy he had liked the paper when he first read it and it wasn't until he heard Morrell's mystical explanation that he was a smart enough politician to see that this wouldn't go down in that form, or help him in his battle between the Home Office and the social services departments. Jim said he would produce a paper of his own and I gather that his intention is to keep Morrell out of it as far as he can. [Crossman, 1977, p. 139]

When we seek the origins of the CDP, then, it is clear that the initiative did not come, in the first instance, from politicians. Equally, there is little evidence of pressure group interest in, or support for, such a measure, and no evidence that the general public was demanding such a programme. The original scheme for the CDP was, quite distinctly, a creation of the civil service, with Derek Morrell as its chief architect. Whether James Callaghan ever did produce 'a paper of his own' is unclear, but when the official statements about the CDP were first issued the Home Office press releases borrowed verbatim large sections of Morrell's Report for the Inter-departmental Working Party. Years later, when the Home Office was criticized for its paternalist and 'colonialist' attitude towards poor communities, it was Morrell's phraseology in particular that gave offence.

It is important to emphasize the centrality of Morrell's role in the deliberations about the CDP, not only because the blueprint was largely his, but also to underline the significance his premature death, in December 1969, was to have upon the progress of the Project. He has variously been described as a man of 'creative imagination, practical idealism, purposive zest, persuasive ingenuity, compassionate generosity, administrative capacity and inventiveness (*The Times*, 13 December 1969), as 'a person of great power' (*Times Educational Supplement*, 19 December 1969), and as a civil servant who was 'not an agent but a creator of policy' (*New Society*, 18 December 1969. In the year before his death Morrell saw the formal announcement of the Community Development Project (in July 1969) and chaired the Ditchley Conference of that year. He became ill in November and died on 10 December, at the age of 48. *New Society* (18 December 1969), reporting his death, was prophetic on two counts. It described the CDP as 'possibly too adventurous for the government to keep up the effort without a man of Morrell's calibre highly placed inside the machine to press for them', and it observed that the Project had been left at 'a fragile stage'. Just how fragile the coalition of interests united under the CDP banner had become was soon apparent.

Thus far in the development of the CDP the accusations that ministers and civil servants in the Home Office had as their main aim 'a coordinated programme of internal repression and control' (Bridges, 1975, p. 377) seems inappropriate. Where issues of control did arise, they centred around two main themes. The first, and most dominant, was concern over matters of territoriality within central government Departments, while the second involved exercising a benevolent, but paternalistic, influence over families, individuals and communities who were said to be 'malfunctioning'. In the first case there was undeniable conflict over which particular Departments would eventually control the different services and programmes to be redistributed after the Seebohm reorganization of the personal social services. The vague concept of 'community' was clearly something that a number of Departments felt belonged to them.

The recommendation of the Seebohm Committee that the new social services departments would have 'a clear responsibility' (Seebohm Report, 1969, para. 483) for promoting community development was obviously at odds with Morrell's own proprietary interest in the notion. Phoebe Hall reports that some members of the Seebohm Committee saw the new Home Office interest in positive discrimination in deprived communities as raising 'the danger of unplanned overlapping', while others saw it as 'an encroachment upon their terms of reference' (Hall, 1976, p. 67). In the event, it was 'reluctantly agreed' that the Committee should continue its deliberations without further discussions of the Community Development Project. Nevertheless, this still left the question of what was to be done with the probation service and the Children's Department (then located in the Home Office) rather in the air. The somewhat bland references to these matters in the Seebohm Report belie the controversy over issues that as Phoebe Hall (1976) indicates, were in fact 'hotly disputed'. Similarly, Harry Specht claims that

> Some informed observers held the belief that CDP was developed as insurance against the possibility that the Seebohm recommendations would not be implemented while others believed that it was developed by the Home Office as insurance against the possibility that Seebohm was implemented. [Specht, 1976, pp. 7–8]

Others certainly felt that the CDP represented an attempt by Morrell to pre-empt the proposals being formulated by the Seebohm Committee, (Specht, 1976, p. 7–8). Whichever of these interpretations is the more accurate, it was clearly the case that both civil servants and politicians in central government, but particularly in the DHSS and the Home Office, were very much preoccupied with territorial issues - almost, on occasion, to the exclusion of anything else. As far as civil servants were concerned, then, their first priority was not, as some writers have suggested, the control of the working class, or the unemployed, or militant blacks, but a desire to preserve or extend their responsibilities in the wake of the reorganization of social services following the Seebohm Report.

The argument that the location of the CDP within the Home Office represented 'part of a longer-term process involving the centralization of government social control activities' (Bridges, 1975, p. 378) also seems misplaced. It wasn't 'put there' so much as allowed to stay there, in so far as the two civil servants most closely associated with drafting the proposals for the CDP – Derek Morrell and Joan Cooper – were senior members of the Home Office staff. Callaghan's desire, as Home Secretary, to retain the CDP, the Urban Programme and the Children's Department appears not to have been intended to place under one roof the Government's main social control activities, but almost the reverse: he wanted to preserve these commitments in order to off set the essentially negative law and order functions that were inevitably the responsibility of the Home Office. As *The Times* 'Diary' observed on 19 July 1968, Callaghan felt it was 'important for the morale of the Home Office that they should not be stripped of creative social responsibilities and left simply with the regulatory responsibilities which now and then are bound to bring them into the harsh glare of controversy'.

In the second case, it is true that Morrell and others within the Home Office wished to control members of deprived communities in the sense of changing their behaviour. However, in Morrell's eyes at least this was to be done in the interests of the people concerned rather than in the interests of social order (although, in so far as this might result in a reduction of 'anti-social' behaviour and delinquency, the two happily coincided). One can only speculate about Morrell's real intentions, but in all that he wrote he appeared much more concerned with 'social growth' than with 'social control', and with compassion rather than repression. His enthusiasm for promoting 'acceptable' behaviour may have been misplaced, but the indications are that it sprang from benign and not malevolent intentions. As a contributor to *The Times* wrote, 'the objective nearest to his heart was, in his own words, to promote the cooperative development of the services and professions which help people to grow' (*The Times*, 13 December 1969). Whether Morrell was right or wrong in these aims, there was nothing sinister or dishonourable in his plans for community development.

THE FIRST YEARS

In January 1970 the Community Development Project formally came into being. The hiatus between Morrell's death in December 1969 and his replacement by Geoffrey Otton in April 1970 was both embarrassing and damaging. Apart from being faced with a large backlog of work when he took over the direction of the CDP, Otton also had to contend with an impending general election. There was the problem too of the very public debate about the Home Office's failure to provide adequate accommodation for Mary Bell, the young girl who had been convicted of murder and for whom no appropriate residential care existed. From the beginning, the CDP had failed to attract a full complement of staff within the civil service, and this problem was to grow rather than to recede. While Morrell had been Under Secretary he had no Assistant Secretary, and it was John Banks, a Principal on secondment from the DES, who had the main responsibility for the day-to-day running of the Project. John Greve of Southampton University, who was appointed as Research Director within the Home Office and who was to have started work on the Project in May 1969, was almost immediately summoned by Richard Crossman to do urgent research on homelessness. The result was that he spent several days a week between May

1969 and June 1970, and half his time between September and December 1970, on the work for Crossman.

It quickly became apparent that the early enthusiasm for the CDP when it was first planned in 1968 could not be sustained. Derek Morrell and Joan Cooper had both been quite fully occupied, during 1969, in steering the Children and Young Persons Act through its final stages in legislation. There is even the suggestion that Morrell was, in any case, beginning to tire of the CDP. Being essentially an 'ideas man', it is claimed, he began to lose interest in the Project when it got through to the detailed planning phase. Civil servants in other departments claimed that there was no real interest in joint planning or coordination either, once the initial interest had waned. By early 1970, then, a good deal of the original momentum had already been lost.

In the meantime, considerable controversy – and in some cases acrimony – had arisen over the choice of areas for CDP resources. Late in 1969 the Cabinet had specified a number of criteria that should be used to determine their selection. These included requirement to have a geographical spread of projects so that each of the major regions – London, the South, the West Midlands, the North (or North-East), Wales and Scotland – would each have at least one project team. They recommended that some of the projects should be located outside the large cities, but also that the list should include one of the 'better-known or tough areas of high social need', such as Notting Hill, St Anne's (Nottingham). Sparkbrook (Birmingham) or Glasgow. Furthermore, they suggested that at least one of the areas should be 'identifiably immigrant'. Finally, the CDP was encouraged to look for ways of breaking new ground in areas where there was no history of voluntary effort. However, there were differences of opinion over whether the primary objective of the CDP should be to work in areas that were well provided with services, to see where improvements might be made, or to focus upon areas deprived of voluntary and statutory support, to test out the possible regenerative effects of injecting small amounts of money. Certainly the Central Steering Group had argued in 1969 that: 'The Project is not set up to demonstrate what can be done in an area which is very poorly provided with services, but to find out what new solutions can be attempted successfully when services are good' (Home Office, unpublished memo, 1969). In at least one case, however, an area was actually disqualified from participating in the CDP because its services were efficient and well developed, on the grounds that it would be a pity to impose on an area, from outside, a project that might stifle the incentive already being displayed.

More often, it was a clash of personalities that inhibited the speedy establishment of local teams in areas across the country. Many of those responsible for impeding progress seemed to come from two groups: elected representatives in the local authorities, and academics within the universities or polytechnics who had been approached to take over responsibility for research. In two cases extremely protracted negotiations (which were almost a full-time commitment for the civil servant involved) eventually came to nothing, and new discussions had to be started with other areas, other institutions and other individuals. Members of some local authorities felt that the Home Office had been insensitive and heavy-handed in its attempts to establish local projects. In Glyncorrwg, for example, which did in fact become one of the first areas to participate, local councillors complained about the lack of consultation and claimed that, in portraying their areas as socially deprived, the Home Office had blackened their image. Councillor Edgar Lewis said that press reports of deprivation in the area gave the impression that people were 'a lot of hill-billies': 'We are hoping to attract new industry to this area,' he went on, 'but how are we going to do so now?' Similarly, Councillor Davies complained, 'We do not live in a human jungle up here, but are human beings who look after the interests of other people' (*South Wales Echo*, 25 February 1970).

The question of what the local action and research team should actually be doing seemed to get overlooked in the race to get first one set of projects off the ground and then another. It was during this important formative period that the seeds of discontent were sown among the local teams, especially with respect to their relations with the Home Office. They received what they regarded as insufficient support and guidance, and Home Office interest (not surprisingly, given the problems of staffing) seemed to be restricted to 'crisis intervention' with those action and research teams which had come into immediate conflict, either with each other or with their local authorities. A further issue arising out of this period of ambiguity and uncertainty was also to have a lasting impact upon the design of the CDP: this was the focus upon 'social pathology' as the main research theme.

Although an early document on research strategy in the CDP advised local teams to look at a broad range of socioeconomic determinants of deprivation (unemployment rates, housing stock, land use and industrial development and demographic factors), it was the emphasis on Morrell's notion of 'individual, family and community malfunctioning' that came to predominate. In drawing up community profiles of their areas, teams quickly came to resist – and resent – the implication that poverty and deprivation could be explained through behavioural factors (drunkenness, alcoholism, absenteeism) at the individual level. Such resentment arose, at least in part, out of a series of unintended developments and misunderstandings. First of all, Morrell's reports for the Inter-departmental Working Party (from which many of the early CDP guidelines derived) were not intended to be a blueprint for a poverty programme. Morrell's original conception had been of something altogether more modest – an 'experiment in social growth'. It was individual self-improvement that interested him, not solving major problems of deprivation. Second, civil servants issuing these guidelines to local teams claim to have seen them simply as that: a guide to the kind of approaches that might be taken, but which may or may not be relevant, and which had to be tested empirically. One Home Office document issued in 1970, for example, emphasized that it was 'not seeking to impose an inflexible or inappropriate research framework on individual teams', while another, in the same year, declared: 'The procedure described here must not, of course, be allowed to become a Procrustean bed, impeding the team's work by denying them flexibility or the right to change their minds in the light of experience'

(Home Office unpublished memo, 1970). Nevertheless, many of the local teams felt they were being pressured, either directly or indirectly, to seek out pathological behaviour in individuals and to concentrate upon correcting this. Whether the teams were right in this assumption or whether civil servants in the Home Office really did have open minds about the causes and solutions to social problems is a matter of interpreting the written, verbal and other signals that passed between the teams and the Home Office. What is certain is that, from the very beginning, there were several different interpretations of what the CDP was, and what it should be doing to (and for) whom.

While the first four teams were struggling to establish themselves (especially *vis-à-vis* their local authorities), the battle to agree upon a second group of four projects continued. At a Cabinet meeting in April 1970, the criteria for choosing the next project areas were identified (or, in some cases, reaffirmed). The Cabinet wished to see a geographical spread of projects and a mix of urban and rural locations. They also reiterated their earlier point that the quality of existing local services should be an important determinant; they were looking particularly for social services and education departments that might be expected to be cooperative. Finally, and presumably because difficulties were already being experienced on this score, they were looking for areas where the local university could be relied upon for support. At the same time, however, they wished to limit the number of university towns involved, and cities such as Nottingham and Leicester were excluded from consideration on this basis. Certain other areas, such as Camden and Sheffield, were also excluded, on the grounds that they were involved in other experiments or research projects or that voluntary effort was already well established. When a short-list of possible areas had been drawn up, exploratory visits were made by civil servants, CDP research staff and, occasionally, ministers in order to reach a final decision.

By now there was some anxiety among civil servants that the whole enterprise was beginning to fall flat, and one advised that it was important to make a public announcement as soon as the next four areas had been chosen – 'in order to maintain interest in the development of the Project (which has been slow in developing momentum during its early stages)'. The situation was aggravated by the fact that the Treasury had turned its attention to the Project and was aiming to reduce the total number of teams from 12 to 10, on the grounds that the projected cost of the CDP had now risen to an unacceptably high level.

Meanwhile, the game of musical chairs, involving civil servants responsible for the CDP, continued. The post of Assistant Secretary, which had been vacant, was filled, initially on a part-time basis, by Donald Morrison, who was in fact located elsewhere, and for whom the CDP was only one of a number of responsibilities. In June 1970 John Banks was recalled to the DES and was not replaced until November 1970, when Robin Birch was transferred from the DHSS. In January 1971 Geoffrey Otton was replaced, as Under Secretary, by Sandy Isserlis (who Crossman describes as 'an inward-looking, persecuted, difficult, learned man': Crossman, 1977, p. 906) who had come from Harold Wilson's staff at 10 Downing St. By this stage the link between the original architects of the CDP and those now responsible for it had effectively been broken. Critics claimed that Isserlis was cynical about the Project (or, at best, uninterested in it), and had thoughts about closing it down. In the event, he left the civil service in March 1972 (and was replaced by Peter Grant, who subsequently died in office).

Although such a high level of mobility is not unusual in the civil service, it was a factor that particularly adversely affected the early development of the CDP. It was exacerbated by the deaths, within a short space of time, of two of the Under Secretaries responsible for the Project, a general election, and the proposed reorganization of social services, the National Health Service and local government. These changes, among others, created feelings of unease and uncertainty, low morale (both inside the Home Office and outside), and a general sense that the civil servants had lost control of (not to say interest in) the Project. The lack of continuity at crucial periods in the planning of the CDP (especially in the last months of 1970) gave rise to problems in the drafting and implementation of policy that were never really overcome.

In a number of respects one can identify two phases in the

development of the CDP, and these problems of ambiguity and uncertainty were characteristic of almost the whole of the first phase, which ran up to the end of 1973 or early 1974. Civil servants were concerned, primarily, with issues arising at central government level. First of all, they had to contend with the question of where the CDP was actually to be located (it eventually became the responsibility of the Community Programmes Department in the Home Office). There was the problem of defining the aims of the CDP with sufficient clarity to enable local teams to begin programmes of action towards those ends. There were the threats from the Treasury of reducing the size of the Project, and even suggestions from those 'within' the CDP that it might either be closed down or have its functions transferred to other departments. Most of all, perhaps, there were the difficulties of encouraging commitment to a project with diffuse aims, little political support and few obvious benefits either to politicians or local authorities – or, indeed, the poor. Throughout this first phase the ever-changing complement of civil servants responsible for the Project had the major task on their hands of simply maintaining its momentum.

Very little was written about the CDP in the early 1970s. It barely attracted the attention of the press (except local newspapers in areas where teams were beginning to make their presence felt), and there were few mentions of it in *Hansard*. Partly in response to this lack of interest in, and lack of information about, the CDP, Ray Lees and George Smith, in 1973, put together a book of readings entitled *Action–Research in Community Development* (which was eventually published in 1975). The cooperative effort between members of different local teams that this book reflected, the earlier establishment of the Consultative Council (in 1972) and the publication of the first Inter-project Report in 1973 marked the end of the first phase of the CDP's development. Clearly, the shift in emphasis in the Project took place over a period of time and cannot be dated precisely. However, a number of changes taking place between 1972 and 1974 signified important adjustments to the original conception of the Project.

THE 'RADICALIZATION' OF THE PROJECT

The turnover of staff within the Home Office, the problems of selecting areas for CDP teams and the preoccupation with heading off crises in one or two of those already chosen meant the (probably unintentional) neglect of most of the local action and research teams. The net effect was that those with responsibility for the CDP in the Home Office failed to provide strong leadership, and for most of its early years the Project was, in many respects, a rudderless ship. Although teams were given advice on administrative and technical details, there was relatively little overall guidance on what the Project as a whole was hoping to achieve, and what their contribution in particular might be. Related to this was the failure to establish a genuinely 'national' programme. Until the local teams took the initiative themselves in setting up the Consultative Council in 1972, there was little inter-project cooperation, and each team was operating in isolation from the others. There had been no effective means of reviewing progress in the local teams, of recording the changes that were taking place there or of learning lessons from similar developments occurring in different areas of the country.

The local teams were frustrated by what they saw as the 'slow and cumbersome' nature of the decision-making process in the CDP. Delay was caused by a number of factors, but not least, as one of the Central Team wrote, by 'memoranda, minutes, official letters, long train journeys, civic lunches and meetings' (unpublished memo). So much effort was invested by civil servants in cultivating the 'right' connections in the localities, and in smoothing over the various conflicts that arose, that the original objectives of the CDP almost disappeared from view. The issue came to a head late in 1971, when a small internal inquiry was launched on the subject of 'lost requests' from the local teams. There had been a number of instances in which the teams had sent requests for help, information or advice up through the CDP structure which appeared to have been lost *en route*. It transpired that many of these involved questions that crossed departmental boundaries and were not clearly the responsibility of one department rather than another. The result, in an unacceptably high number of cases, was that no action was taken, and issues at the local level simply remained unresolved. As Specht has pointed out:

> the impact on the Directors of the lack of inter-agency co-ordination at the Central level was enormous. Those Directors who confronted a local political situation that appeared intractable were, of course, most severely disappointed and angered by the lack of support and follow-through at the center. [Specht, 1976, p. 47]

It was fairly obvious, at this stage, that the conflict between local teams and central authorities was rapidly coming to a head.

In December 1971 a meeting of project directors and the Central Team was held at Dorking, and from this it was clear that the directors wished to take over the coordinating function of the CDP themselves. They proposed the setting up of a Consultative Council which would, in effect, take over the responsibilities of the Central Research Team. The report of the meeting outlines the areas of dissatisfaction expressed by the directors:

> In particular they considered that the Central Team should help local teams to obtain technical expertise more readily than hitherto, especially on the research side, and in the area of action consultancy. As projects developed, Project Directors wished to transmit their experience back to the centre so that they could contribute to the development of national policy within the project and to influencing the development of the policy of other government departments. At present, Project Directors felt that there was insufficient evidence that the practical experience of CDP was modifying national policy in an acceptable way, e.g. in relation to the implications of experience with difficult local authorities for policy toward future CDP areas. [meeting at Wotton Hall, Dorking, 7–8 December, Consultative forum: Home Office, 18 February 1972]

By 1972, therefore, a number of factors had contributed towards a changing emphasis within the Project. Up to this point the main focus of activity had lain within central government. However, when the choice of all 12 areas had been accomplished in 1972, and with the running down of the Central Research Unit, attention switched to the activities of the project teams in their own communities. In April 1972 John Greve resigned as Research Director of the CDP and his post became redesignated that of Research Consultant, carrying with it fewer responsibilities. On 28 May Reginald Maudling (then Home Secretary) announced in the House of Commons that there would be less central control generally over the Project, and that local teams themselves would be expected to take the initiative. Approval was formally given to the establishment of the Consultative Council and to a new Information and Intelligence Unit, which was to be based at the Centre for Environmental Studies. It was expected that the Consultative Council would provide a forum for discussions between members of local teams, civil servants, what remained of the Central Research Team and other interested parties. Although the Home Office retained formal control over the 12 teams and administrative responsibility for them, it was to the Consultative Council that project directors and team members now turned as their main reference point. The establishment of the Council thus marked a significant turning point in the development of the CDP and resulted from the growing assertiveness, even militancy, of local teams. However, as Harry Specht discovered from his interviews with 'informed observers', it was not universally acclaimed as a step forward. One, at least, regarded it as a 'phyrric victory' for the project directors who, it was claimed, had 'bullied the Home Office staff into submission', but in doing so had cut themselves off from powerful support within central government, (Specht, 1976, pp. 60–1).

If the Home Office was suspicious and the local teams dissatisfied with the progress of the CDP thus far, John Greve, as outgoing Research Director, also had his reservations. In an article in the *Community Development Journal*, he argued that the CDP still lacked 'a clearly defined set of operation objectives' as well as 'genuine coordinating machinery' for the

Project as a whole. The important task of collating and interpreting data from the local teams could not, he argued, be
performed adequately on an ad hoc basis. The failure to set up
appropriate machinery to monitor and evaluate progress on a
systematic basis was, in John Greve's view, the result of a
particular 'culture' within the civil service:

> The tolerant pragmatic ethos of administrative traditions
> in the British civil service creates a climate in which
> something as unconventional as CDP can be sponsored
> and financed. At the same time, this pragmatism, which
> springs in part from enlightened belief in the value of
> gifted individualism, . . . militates against the fashioning
> of organizational arrangements to co-ordinate aims, pro-
> cesses and resources within CDP or the fashioning of inter-
> departmental machinery to maximise the effectiveness of
> the experiment. [Greve, 1973, p. 125]

Three years into the Project, then, criticisms of the way in
which the CDP had developed ranged across a number of issues
and came from several quarters. It came from civil servants
within the Home Office, from members of the Central
Research Team, and from project directors and members of
the local teams, as well as from elected representatives and
residents of CDP areas. The growing consciousness of what the
CDP was doing, and could be doing, was assisted by the steady
increase in the numbers of pamphlets, reports and articles
emanating from the teams. It was the Coventry project, in
particular, having been one of the first to get off the ground
(and to have done so with relative ease), that gave the lead to
new, and more radical, thinking in the CDP.

The Coventry team had begun in 1970, with Home Office
guidelines that owed much to Derek Morrell's original
conception of the nature and causes of individual and
community 'malfunctioning'. However, in translating Morrell's somewhat mystical ideas into a programme of action, the
Home Office had adopted a distinct view of 'social pathology'
which Morrell may not have shared. When John Benington was
appointed as director of the Coventry project, it was

anticipated that he would lead a team including a psychiatric social worker, child care officer, education welfare officer, disablement resettlement officer and a mental welfare officer. The particular brief to the Coventry CDP of developing the personal social services owed a good deal, it is argued, to the fact that the Town Clerk of the day, Sir Charles Barratt, was a member of the Seebohm Committee. It was clear, Benington observed, that the problems were seen as those of 'social cripples and lame ducks' (Lees and Smith, 1975, p. 174). Within two years he and his colleagues had concluded that the problems of their area could not simply be attributed to individual inadequacy or to a deterioration in 'the patterns of community life'. Similarly, Benington argued, 'the solutions for Hillfields could not be looked for in stronger doses of the medicine that the welfare state had been serving up, or in a better mixing of ingredients in the dose' (Lees and Smith, p. 176). By 1972, therefore, the Coventry team was arguing that the CDP should shift its attention from the symptoms of deprivation, and its victims, to its causes. It was a change of emphasis that has been characterized as moving from a 'social pathology' approach to a 'structural' analysis of social problems.

Benington argued that there were essentially three different ways of viewing social problems. The first focused upon families with 'special personal handicaps or peculiar personal pathologies'; the second upon 'maladministration or imperfect planning'; and the third looked for causal factors - in the 'fluctuating relationship between private capital and the state' (Lees and Smith, 1975, p. 182). In its second phase of development, from 1972 onwards, the Coventry team looked particularly to the third area for explanations of the economic decline and deprivation in the part of the city in which team members were based. It led them to examine patterns of investment in industry and their effects on land use and housing, as well as demographic factors and labour market participation. Most of the other teams who submitted progress reports to the Minister responsible for the CDP in 1972 had reached similar conclusions. By the time the first Inter-Project report was prepared in 1973, all hints of a 'social pathology' approach had disappeared. In fact, the Report specifically rejected 'psychological motivations' and 'internal factors' as causes of deprivation, and preferred instead to look at 'structural constraints' and 'external factors' (CDP, 1974, p.8). However the Home Office now viewed the activities of the CDP, the teams themselves (or at least the majority of them) had shifted ground considerably and saw their role as being much more radical than was originally envisaged. The somewhat conventional social work perspective with which many of them began had now been rejected in favour of strategies that focused upon problems of unemployment, housing and the environment, industry and planning, education and income maintenance and upon issues of communication, rights, accountability, power and control. The teams had also concluded that the problems they identified were symptoms of much more deeply rooted inequalities in the distribution of resources and opportunities, which were not peculiar to their neighbourhoods but were of national origin.

From this point, the further radicalization of the CDP can be attributed to a number of factors of varying significance. On the one hand, there were the 'internal' factors, which included the lack of Home Office interest in, and control of, the CDP, changing perceptions of the nature and causes of deprivation, the increasing hostility of the Home Office and some local authorities to local teams the involvement of 'activists' in local teams, and the flow of critical literature on the CDP and its strategies. 'External' factors included an increase in unemployment, cuts in public expenditure, the election of a Conservative government and the introduction of 'regressive' policies, such as the 1972 Housing Finance Act. It is clearly difficult, in looking for the reasons for the 'radicalization' of the CDP, to separate the internal from the external influences on the Project, since the two were often intimately linked. There are, however, two 'internal' factors that seem to have been particularly important in accounting for changes in the direction of the CDP: the personnel involved, and the kind of literature they were producing.

From its inception the CDP had tended – quite predictably – to attract staff who were not in the mould of conventional social workers. Some had backgrounds in community work and organization, while others were qualified in law and social planning. The educational backgrounds of the rest, according to Specht, were in such fields as 'medieval languages, history, philosophy and economics' (1976, p. 3). Applicants for posts in the CDP, in the early days, tended to be disaffected social workers or probation officers, who were frustrated by the constraints of their present jobs and were looking for something new. Many of them saw the CDP as an adventurous and imaginative alternative, even if (or, perhaps, because) it was not clear exactly where the Project was heading. As Martin Loney points out, there was another group of recruits to the CDP who had more firmly established radical credentials. Some of them had been involved in student politics, while others had worked in CND and the peace movement. Probably the best known of this group was John O'Malley, who had worked as a community organizer in Notting Hill and who, according to Loney, was seeking 'a wider constituency than that available in the peace campaign'. These activists, in Loney's view, saw in the CDP 'the opportunity to continue radical community organizing with government paid salaries and government resources' (1981, p. 58). Early on, then, many CDP workers had a predisposition towards 'unconventional' tactics in dealing with social problems.

As one of Specht's informed observers' put it:

> Traditional social work strategies were certainly not ruled out from the range of strategies which might be pursued. But most of the participants in CDP . . . were attracted to community work because they held a standpoint which, if not hostile to traditional social work to begin with, certainly developed a hostility in the course of their work. [Specht, 1976, p. 26]

Such a position was almost certain to bring CDP workers into conflict with their employing authorities and, in a number of cases, quickly did so. One newspaper report claimed that in Cleator Moor, for example, 'The council officers found the CDP's left-wing, alternative ideas upsetting, and the office was soon labelled the little Moscow; their information centre, the Kremlin' (*Observer* Magazine, 16 March 1975). In Southwark, shortly after taking office, the action team director became aware that: 'some of the Council's members and officers had reservations ranging from scepticism to explicit opposition regarding the local project and about some of the ideas on which she believed community development to be based' (Hatch *et al.*, 1977, p. 98); while in Batley, local councillors were said to oppose the 'commitment to militant action on behalf of the poor' displayed by some CDP workers (*Community Care, 2 October 1974*).

As the local teams acquired a reputation for militancy and radicalism, so they tended to attract more activists to them – with a series of dramatic outcomes. The first of these was the announcement, in June 1974, that the Home Office was to conduct a 'Management Review' of the CDP. Its brief was to 'examine the organisation, structure and method of operation of the Community Development Project, and advise the Home Office of any changes that might improve its effectiveness' (Lees and Smith, 1975, p. viii). Despite the blandness of this announcement, many CDP workers interpreted it as a move to find ways of pruning – or even terminating – the Project, and of heading off some of its radical tendencies. Corkey and Craig observe that 'it was about this time that a Cabinet minute noted concern over the growing "political" content of CDP and suggested that closer monitoring would be useful' (1978, p. 65). Whatever was intended by the Management Review, it had the effect of creating tension and uncertainty among members of local teams, and produced suspicion and hostility all round.

Second came the strike, and subsequent resignation, of four community workers in the Batley CDP in July, 1974. In a statement issued to the press they alleged that many people now saw the CDP as 'an example of maximum political concern at minimum cost, as a piece of window dressing' (statement by CDP community workers, 1 July 1974.) They claimed that they were being prevented from doing the job they had been engaged to do because of interference from their employers. The issue centred upon the use of 'social action money', which the local authority insisted upon controlling, but which the local team felt should have been allocated without restrictions on its use. The resignation of the four Batley workers was followed by that of the director of the project, Paul Henderson, in October 1975. He had been asked to resign by Kirklees Council, which claimed that he had been unfairly critical of them. He was phlegmatic about his dismissal and observed: 'When I took over the job, people warned me that it was the most impossible job in the country – they were right' (*Community Care*, 15 October 1975).

A third development was the establishment, also in 1974, of the Political Economy Collective (PEC) and the CDP Workers' Organization (CDPWO). According to Corkey and Craig (1978), the aim of the PEC was that of 'analysing and publicising processes in project areas through a Marxist political economy approach', while CDPWO was seen as a substitute for the Consultative Council, which in their view (one that was not universally shared) was now regarded 'as merely a token gesture at democratising CDP' (p. 50). Both of these moves were a far cry from the way in which Morrell (and others in the Home Office) had envisaged the CDP developing, and illustrated the rapidity with which the Project had become 'radicalized'.

The period of uncertainty for CDP workers did not come to an end with the publication of the results of the Management Review late in 1974. Indeed, shortly afterwards the Home Office announced that there would be cuts in expenditure on the CDP and a moratorium on new appointments. This was followed, some time later, by a report in the *Sunday Times* that claimed that the Government was 'quietly turning its back on one of Britain's biggest and most radical attempts to fight poverty and deprivation'; that some local authorities were 'only too glad to get rid of what they see as radical-minded activists'; and that 'Whitehall officals will not be sorry to see the projects dying a quiet death one by one'. The CDP, the report concluded, was about to 'face extinction' (*Sunday Times*, 19 October, 1975). The predicted death of the CDP proved to be a little premature, but the final closure of the Information and Intelligence Unit in September 1976 (after two reprieves) was another body blow, and from then on the end was quite definitely in sight.

The second 'internal' factor that had given a boost to the

'radicalization' of the CDP was the volume and nature of the literature beginning to be produced by local teams. As we argued earlier in this chapter, there was a very real concern around 1970–72 that the CDP might simply disintegrate because of the lack of interest in it and lack of information about it. Once the Information and Intelligence Unit (IIU) had been established in 1973, however, there was a concerted attempt by the local teams to reach as wide an audience as possible with their publications. Some of these efforts were frustrated through practical problems of distribution. It was never easy to locate or buy CDP publications, because the responsibility for distributing them shifted from one institution to another, because many bookshops did not stock them, and because libraries tended to catalogue them under a number of different headings rather than as a collection.

Despite these difficulties, the IIU was successful in producing, and selling, a series of national reports including *The Poverty of the Improvement Programme* (CDP 1975). *Whatever Happened to Council Housing?* (CDP , 1976a), and *Profits against Houses* (CDP, 1976b). The most controversial report, however, was that entitled *Cutting the Welfare State (Who Profits?* (CIS/CDP 1975), which was produced jointly by the IIU and Counter Information Services who, as Martin Loney observes, had 'an established background of high quality radical exposes' (1981, p. 58). It was one of the first of a series of direct and radical attacks on the Labour government and its public expenditure programme. The report was significant in its attempt to analyse poverty from the other end of the telescope. In other words, it focused upon the rich, and upon the financial institutions that helped to maintain the degrees of inequality evident in Britain at the time. At the same time, it outlined what it described as 'a scenario of waste and destruction' (CIS/CDP, 1975, p. 39) in the public sector, and did not shrink from attributing blame to the calculated economic and social policies of successive governments – Tory and Labour alike. It was a hard-hitting, persuasive and detailed report, and it is hardly surprising that the Home Office was reluctant to have its name associated with it. The eventual response of the Home Office, two months after the publication of the report (in January 1976), was to announce that the IIU was to be closed down within three months. It claimed that the reports were now becoming 'too political', and there is no doubt that they looked very different from most of the literature receiving the Home Office imprimatur. In the event, and after opposition from a number of sources, the Unit won a reprieve until September 1976. Two other major reports, *The Costs of Industrial Change* (CDP, 1977a) and *Gilding the Ghetto* (CDP, 1977b), were already in the pipeline and eventually emerged in 1977. It was the second of these that attracted most attention, and it probably remains one of the most widely read of all CDP publications.

By the time *Gilding the Ghetto* was in production, a number of those responsible for writing the CDP reports had concluded that the civil servants, politicians and academics whom they had been addressing comprised the wrong audience. There was a conscious attempt with this latest report, then, to produce something that was simply written and attractively presented (with more photographs), and would appeal to a wider public. *Gilding the Ghetto* set the CDP in the context of a series of government initiatives to deal with the 'urban crisis', 'pockets of poverty' and inner-city decline. It argued that, through inadequate resources, a failure to identify the real causes of deprivation and a lack of political commitment, these projects had been singularly ineffective. They should be seen, it claimed, more as aspects of a broader policy of social control, and as cosmetic exercises, rather than as serious attempts to tackle inequality and deprivation. In Liverpool, for example, the considerable number of poverty projects (including an estimated 146 urban aid schemes), from the CDP and the EPA onwards, had noticeably failed to affect basic problems of housing, employment and so on. In fact, during the early 1970s unemployment increased rapidly, council house building declined, and the payment of improvement grants decreased dramatically. Nationally, too, while the 12 local teams were attempting to effect improvements in social conditions, unemployment was rising (from 3.4 per cent in 1971 to 6 per cent in 1977), homelessness was increasing, the real value of welfare benefits was declining, and public expenditure was being reduced. The conclusion of *Gilding the Ghetto* was that, in the light of these developments, the government was really seeking – in the CDP – a means of managing the poor, rather than of eradicating deprivation.

While these national reports attempted to integrate the experiences in different parts of the country, local teams continued to produce a series of leaflets and pamphlets describing conditions in their areas. Totalling more than 200, these various publications provide a detailed picture of poverty, its causes, and the effects of policies to deal with it. Although the picture is far from complete, it takes in a wide variety of issues, and together these reports make up one of the most comprehensive surveys of poverty ever undertaken in Britain. With the closure of the IIU in 1976, however, the opportunity for collating these data was lost, and the momentum for a change in policy at central government level evaporated. The amount of knowledge accumulated in the various research projects under the aegis of the CDP was considerable, and the fact that it was seen as being of only local importance is perhaps one of the greatest losses of the CDP exercise. The financial implications of taking on board all the recommendations of the reports obviously meant that government had a vested interest in adopting this approach, however. The Urban Deprivation Unit, in the Home Office, continued to publish and distribute CDP reports after the closure of the IIU, but this was more of a 'holding operation' than an attempt to breathe new life into the central organization of the project.

The closure of the IIU marked the beginning of the end for the CDP. It had always been envisaged that the local projects would have a limited life-span (of five years), but the final stages of the Programme came more quickly than many had anticipated. By the end of 1976 two of the projects (in Cleator Moor and Batley) had closed prematurely because of local difficulties. The local authorities in which they were based had, it appeared, gratefully slipped through the loop hole created in the widely publicized letter of October 1975. In this the Home Office had advised local authorities that if – given the unfavourable economic climate – they felt unable to maintain their commitment to the local projects, the Home Office would accept proposals for their closure. The remaining ten projects drew to a staggered conclusion, most of them by 1978, with little fanfare or comment.

CDP: POLITICS OR POLICY?

The question that remains is whether the CDP was really a crudely assembled package designed to deal with a number of specific political problems, or was genuinely intended to confront a range of policy issues in an experimental, but systematic, form. The answer is that it was probably expected to achieve both ends – an example of what S. M. Miller has described in the American context as 'cost-free liberalism'. It is also true that different interest groups had many different expectations of the projects. The 'political' intentions of civil servants in the Home Office, for example, were not necessarily those of their political masters, or of members of the local authorities or radical activists in local teams.

As far as the political aims of the CDP were concerned, the growing unease about immigration after the publication of the Race Relations Bill in 1968, exacerbated by the inflammatory speeches of Enoch Powell, was certainly a subject of serious concern to the government of the day. However, it was largely an accident of timing that Morrell's proposals for community action areas arrived on the desk of his minister at the same time as the government was beginning to search around for ways of responding to mounting criticisms of its various domestic policies. If the proposals had not existed, it would almost certainly have been necessary to invent them. As it was, Morrell's was a conveniently inexpensive, and relatively well thought through, package which could be pushed forward as a temporary expedient to pacify the critics who argued that the government 'must act'. The timing of the first planning phases of the CDP (described in an earlier section) were such that the Project cannot simply be seen as a hasty response to Powell's speech of 20 April 1968. By that stage, it was already on the stocks and had been drafted in some detail. The fact that it moved so quickly from idea to reality, however, no doubt owed a good deal to 'political necessity'.

The related question of whether the CDP (and its location in the Home Office) was part of some grand design to 'incorporate protest' raises some interesting issues. It is an irony that the CDP (like its American predecessors) was itself responsible – to a significant degree – for creating the conditions that gave rise to the need for an element of control by government. In other words, in 1969, when the Project began, there was little evidence in the 12 chosen areas of actual or potential social unrest. Most of them, especially Birmingham and Coventry, had a higher than average concentration of immigrants (which may have been thought to increase their volatility), but this did not, in practice, appear to lessen their stability. As far as one can ascertain, they were, on the whole, deprived, somewhat passive communities, with no real history of violent protest. The more widespread dissent engendered in the early 1960s by students and by the peace movement had more or less passed them by. By 1978, in contrast, by which time most of the local teams had been withdrawn, there had been rent strikes, organized opposition to the 1972 Housing Finance Bill, welfare rights campaigns, demonstrations and squatting. In short, there was a much greater need (from the perspective of government) for measures of control in the 12 areas when the teams left than there had been before they arrived. This must be attributed, in part, to the consciousness-raising activities of the local teams, who tended to arouse strong feelings rather than to repress them, as may originally have been envisaged by the Home Office. These developments should however, be seen in the context of an increased willingness, nationally, to engage in direct action, in the form of strikes, sit-ins, picketing and the like.

Although there were some observers in 1968–69 who had seen the potential for a degree of 'social control' in the CDP, the control issue did not fully arise until four or five years later. By the mid-1970s superficial analysis would suggest that there was not only a greater necessity for the damping down of protest in deprived communities (whose needs were becoming more forcefully articulated), but also more evidence that the Home Office was anxious to control the activities of the projects to which it had given life. Perhaps the most controversial aspect of Home Office (and, in some cases, local authority) policy was the extent to which it attempted to determine not only what members of the local teams did, but also what they said, both in words and in print. Although the boundaries of acceptable behaviour were never clearly drawn, agencies of central and local government reacted quickly when they considered the local teams to have transgressed them. As the *Guardian* observed, in 1975, their responses tended to look like those of 'bureaucratic infanticide upon an unruly child' (3 January 1975). The political elements of social control in the CDP, then, shifted, to some extent, from a concern with external to internal factors. In 1968 the problem for the Home Office was crime, urban decay and immigration, in 1974 it was also the CDP. Obviously, this is an oversimplification of the pressures at work, and if the fate of the CDP was an urgent matter to those working in it, it was only one of a series of problems with which the Home Office had to deal. On the national scene the CDP was of only minor importance. It was no more than an irritating sore for the Home Office, and politically it continued to be more or less a non-issue. Nevertheless, it can probably be argued that a policy innovation that was seen, to a limited degree, as having functions of control (in terms of 'gilding the ghetto' or 'buying time', as Joan Cooper put it), itself became an object of control over a period of years, and the issue became one essentially of 'guarding the guards'.

Finally, in so far as the CDP was intended to deal with a number of policy problems, it is generally regarded as having been unsuccessful. Brynmor John, M.P. for example, in announcing the termination of the Project in the House of Commons, claimed that it had had 'a negative result' and that it had principally taught the government 'what not to do', rather than what to do (*Hansard*, 17 November 1977). While acknowledging that negative lessons were sometimes valuable, he remained unenthusiastic about the outcome of the CDP. Many of those involved in writing the more than 200 reports, on the other hand, would argue that – on the contrary – they had spelled out many lessons for policy and could prescribe courses of action that governments who seriously wished to reduce poverty might follow.

The failure of the CDP to make a more positive impact is

often attributed to the death of its chief advocate, Derek Morrell, at an early stage in its development. The implication of this is that the CDP would have been more successful if he had lived. Is the assumption justified? It is justified in the sense that Morrell may have been successful in engineering greater political support for the Project, which, in the event, was noticeably lacking. He would also have been able to translate, to those who were interested, what the CDP was actually about. After his death there was never any real agreement about the concept and aims of the Project and it was in great need of a spokesman, especially in the early years. Without Morrell the CDP was like a ship without a navigator. She continued to sail, but with different individuals at the helm and with no clear idea of her course. On the other hand, as we have suggested earlier, there are also grounds for believing that Morrell was more interested in the ideas behind the CDP than in their execution, and that, when he died, his interest in the Project was already beginning to wane. There is also John Greve's observation that the civil service, generally, is more successful in generating innovations than in implementing them. It was the implementation stage of the CDP that was crucial, and where many good ideas foundered. As James Callaghan remarked in the House of Commons, 'its fate lay more in the hands of those who carried it out, than in the mind of the originator' (*Hansard*, 14 July 1977). One could, of course, argue that good ideas cannot really be regarded as good if they are not capable of implementation. However, many of the CDP's early intentions, such as better coordination of services and careful experimentation, seemed sound enough in principle and, given more favourable conditions, might have worked in practice. As it was, there was no sustained attempt to confront inter-departmental rivalries either in central or local government. It would have taken more than a handful of civil servants, and a much stronger Central Steering Group, to override the powerful interests in Whitehall and to enforce some degree of coordination. However, it quickly became apparent that, while there was some commitment, in principle, to the idea of coordination, no one, in practice, wished to fight the battle. As far as 'controlled experimentation' was concerned, some at least of the difficulties encountered in translating the idea into action could have been avoided. The problems of securing research support from 'nearby institutions', and of ensuring that action teams and research teams began together, should not, in principle, have been insoluble (although, in practice, they proved extremely difficult to settle). At the same time, the conflict between the 'political' and 'policy' aims of the CDP were nowhere more apparent than in the experimental aspects of the programme. The CDP as a political initiative required that ends remain unspecific and relatively ambiguous, so that there was the possibility of obtaining wide political support, while – in contrast – the policy intentions of the programme demanded that a clear cut statement of ends, means and resources be made explicit. The need for ambiguity in one case and its undesirability in the other made the political and policy aims of the Project somewhat incompatible. Ambiguity let the 'radicals' in and hereby, some would argue, spelled its demise. However, as long as there were differences of opinion about the direction in which the Project should be heading, it was as legitimate for the radicals to leap on board and take the helm as for any other interest group to do so.

It is not unreasonable to conclude that the CDP was the wrong programme, dealing with the wrong problem in the wrong way. However, in the various assessments of the Project now available, its limitations have tended to be emphasized at the expense of its achievements. The CDP did not have the economic resources to effect a major reduction in the incidence of poverty, or the political resources to achieve a fundamental, and more favourable, shift in poverty policy. Its successes were on a much more modest scale, but they were real nevertheless. First, it made available a mass of data on economic and social decline in different areas of the country, on the impact of social services, and on the economic, political and industrial influences that contributed to the pauperization of towns and cities and their inhabitants. So far these data have been very much under-utilized, primarily because of problems of access to them, but also because there has been no overall attempt to draw them together, and indeed no final report on the CDP experience as a whole.

A second success of the Project lies in its educational functions. It provided a valuable test-bed for activists of many persuasions, illustrating the potential and limitations of different forms of social action. For those employed in the programme it was an exercise in inter-group relations as well as in politics and diplomacy. For the people in many of the CDP areas it showed what tactics might be useful, for what purposes.

Finally, the CDP has contributed to policy change, to a limited degree, through a process of osmosis. Like a good deal of similar policy research, it has helped to modify ideas, not directly so much as by helping to change the 'climate of opinion'. Perceptions change by the passage of ideas through 'semi-permeable membranes' and gradually, and almost imperceptibly, have their effects on policy. It is difficult to see this process in operation over a short time span, so that experiments in 'social growth', such as the CDP, almost inevitably seem failures when evaluated at the end of their experimental period. It is only with hindsight that we begin to see these changes more clearly. The initiatives described in this book represent, over a 14-year period, an important shift in emphasis. While the CDP began with a belief in individual pathology as a major cause of social problems, the later projects had moved towards a consideration of structural factors and deprivation. The CDP, on its own, cannot take the credit for this change in emphasis, and governments may still revert to the 'pathological approach' on occasions. Indeed, as the recent analyses of the rioting in Toxteth, Brixton, Southall, Moss Side and elsehere show, government ministers are still very ready to blame 'bad parenting' and similar individualistic factors. However, the change in the climate of opinion, to which the CDP contributed, makes it increasingly difficult – in the longer term – to sustain such arguments, and considerable evidence (much of it with the Home Office imprimatur) can now be marshalled to question their validity.

3

The Urban Programme

The most surprising thing about the Traditional Urban Programme in 1981 is that it still exists. Along with the Community Development Project, it ushered in, in the 1960s, a decade of new policies directed specifically at the inner cities and other areas designated as having more than their fair share of urban problems. A decade later, the late 1970s saw the responsibility for urban deprivation policies shift from the Home Office to the Department of the Environment (DOE). With the subsequent emergence of a battery of new policy initiatives, and a reformulation of the nature and causes of urban deprivation, it might have been expected that the Urban Programme would have been made redundant by the new and larger-scale policies. That it survived the post-1977 reorganization is however a tribute less to its efficacy as a policy than to its comprehensive presentational capacities and potential. It cannot be said that the Urban Programme at present achieves a great deal, but its political usefulness is undiminished.

Since there has been some confusion over terminology, it is important at the outset to make clear what is being referred to in this chapter as the 'Traditional Urban Programme'. From 1968, when it was established, until 1978, the Urban Programme constituted a set of arrangements for the part-funding by central government of projects in any local authority in England and Wales[1] that could demonstrate 'special social need' – usually interpreted as some form of urban deprivation or related problem. The Community Development Project was administratively and functionally separate from the Urban Programme but was funded from it. In 1978 the Programme was greatly enlarged, and its various components (some of which had been added in the mid- to late 1970s) more clearly distinguished. From then on, the term 'Urban Programme' became the generic name for, and source of funds of, the Partnership arrangements, the Programme authorities and all other authorities in that order of importance. Thus, the seven (now six)[2] Partnership authorities, deemed to be those with the most urban problems, took the lion's share of Urban Programme funds; the 14 'second-tier deprivation' authorities took the next largest share; and most of the remainder was to be distributed to all other authorities under arrangements similar to those that had existed since 1968. This third component of the Urban Programme became known as the 'Traditional Urban Programme'. It is still referred to in government circulars, however, simply as the 'Urban Programme'. This chapter is about the Traditional Urban Programme, but the shorter term is preferred except where possible confusion requires the use of the full title.

The purpose of this chapter is to examine the Urban Programme in the context of the changes in policy direction and conception of urban deprivation over the past 20 years or so, with a view to assessing the extent to which it has been evaluable and evaluated and has produced knowledge, expertise and experience that have contributed to a linear development of thinking about inner-city policies.

URBAN PROGRAMME 1967–78

The Urban Programme consists essentially of an arrangement by which central government pays a grant at the rate of 75 per cent towards the cost of projects established by local authorities or voluntary agencies in areas of 'special social need'.[3] Local authorities, and through them voluntary organizations, submit details of projects they would wish to establish to the

DOE (until 1976 to the Home Office) in response to annual central government circulars. A selection of these submissions is approved and grant is paid at the rate of 75 per cent for the life of loan charges for capital expenditure and for five years in the first instance for revenue projects. The range of types of projects funded is detailed later in the chapter. The main explicit thrust of the programme has always been the alleviation of urban deprivation or stress in areas of special social need[4] by supplementing main programmes and filling gaps left by them, but it has also always had a special concern with immigrant areas and ethnic minorities. This emphasis of the programme however has always been an uneasy one, and has varied in the degree of explicitness with which it has been promoted. The reasons for this lie in the formative days of the programme and, indeed, in the events leading up to the announcement of its establishment on 5 May 1968.

It is generally acknowledged that there were four major influences on the genesis of the Urban Programme: the 'rediscovery of poverty' and the re-emergence of selectivity in the early and mid-1960s; the American War on Poverty programmes; the growing emphasis on area-specific policies associated with a number of reports published in the 1960s; and the debate about and growing public concern over the issue of immigration and the (mainly) governmental anxiety about race relations from the mid-1950s on. (Hambleton, 1978; Edwards and Batley, 1978; McKay and Cox, 1979; Lawless, 1979, 1981). It is perhaps more accurate to characterize the first three of these as the influencial contexts within which the idea of an urban policy could take root, and the fourth as the immediate stimulus that brought it to fruition.

It is not possible in the space of this chapter to trace these events (which anyway have been extensively mapped elsewhere[5]), but to understand the programme we need to dwell a little on the specific stimulus of immigration and race relations.

The implementation of the Commonwealth Immigration Act in 1962, its interim renewal in 1964 and it extension in 1968 under a Labour Government established the political consensus of the canard that the only way to good race relations was through minimizing the numbers of ethnic minorities. Control came to be seen as (and remains[6]) the orthodox precondition of good race relations, and in large measure subsequent inner-city and race relations policies have been the price we have had to pay for accepting this untruth.

The need for a positive governmental role to balance the controlling legislation was acknowledged in the Race Relations Act of 1965 and its extension in 1968 to cover employment and housing. That these two areas had been dangerous omissions was given force by the results of the major study of discrimination conducted for Political and Economic Planning (Daniel, 1968) and by the study by Burney (1967) of discrimination in the private rented housing market. However, a race relations policy was not sufficient to damp the groundswell of prejudice and discrimination that found 'legitimized' expression in speeches by Enoch Powell, Duncan Sandys and Sir Cyril Osborn. The immediate stimulus for the Urban Programme has been attributed to one particular speech by Mr Powell, though the possibility of some more tangible form of help for immigrant areas had been informally mooted within the Home Office before 20 April 1968. None the less, it remains true that the occasion for the public announcement of the programme was a specific reaction to Mr Powell's speech. In the course of an address delivered in Birmingham on 5 May 1968, Mr Wilson announced that 'we have decided to embark on a new and expanded Urban Programme'. If there is one tangible starting point for Britain's inner-city policies, it was this.

Mr Wilson's announcement came as a surprise to some of the civil servants who were immediately concerned, but it is not true – as has been argued – that it was a bolt out of the blue. The most likely source for the idea that had seeded itself in the Prime Minister's mind was an inter-departmental working party established early in 1968 and chaired by the Home Office, the purpose of which was to review immigration and race relations policy. This working party had considered among other things, the possibility of some form of expenditure programme to further the integration of newly arrived ethnic minorities. One member of that working party later recalled: 'That was, I think, the very first spark'.[7] An idea that may have gestated for months was suddenly precipitated into the policy-making arena by the Prime Minister's intervention.

Mr Wilson placed the responsibility for developing the idea of an Urban Programme with the Home Secretary – not, by today's thinking, the most obvious place for the formulation of an inner-city policy. (The programme and subsequently developed policies were of course to find a new home in the DOE some ten years later.) That the Home Office was chosen as the parent for the programme was due entirely to the immediate context of immigration and race relations issues within which it was conceived, and not, as has been argued, (CDP, 1977b), because it was to be a subtle instrument of social control and hence a component of law and order for which the Home Office carried responsibility.[8] (Also, there was already a precedent within the Home Office in the form of Section 11 Grants under the 1966 Local Government Act – small grants for the payment of additional staff in local authorities with high concentrations of ethnic minorities.)

Two days after the Prime Minister's announcement, a new working party was established that would carry responsibility for developing the programme. It consisted of representatives at Assistant Secretary level from the Ministry of Health and Social Security, the Department of Education and Science, the Department of Employment and Productivity, the Ministry of Housing and Local Government and the Treasury, with the Home Office in the chair. Its terms of reference were:

> to consider implementation of the 'new and expanded Urban Programme' mentioned in the Prime Minister's speech . . . but it would *in addition* serve the interdepartmental committee of officials who were to meet for the first time on 9 May to consider a wide range of subjects affecting areas of immigrant population. [Home office, 1968b].[9]

Its task was a formidable one. It had less than three months (the Prime Minister had expressed the need for urgency) in which to construct the new programme, and precious little to go on by way of guidance either in terms of resources available or aims to be achieved. Such clues as were available to officials were gleaned from Mr Wilson's speech, and these, along with the issues that the Working Party itself considered to be significant, largely determined the form that the programme was to take. It is worth considering these points in a little detail for the light they throw on how the Urban Programme was constructed and why it took the form it did.

From the Prime Minister's speech, the Working Party was able to glean the following salient points:

1   the programme was to be concerned with towns;
2   the problems to which it was to be addressed included education, housing, health and welfare;
3   the context was that of immigration, but 'Expenditure should be on the basis of need, and the immigration problem is only one factor, but a very important factor, in the assessment of social need';
4   there was to be a 'particular emphasis on education . . .';
5   'the Home Secretary will be in charge of working out the details of this programme';
6   'this cost will have to be met within the ceiling of expenditure laid down in the announcement [about general economy measures] I made to Parliament in January'. These ceilings dictated that the programme would have to be financed by redistribution from other sources.

With the benefit of hindsight, however, the *omissions* from the Prime Minister's speech also take on a significance. There was no mention of the problems of unemployment, poverty or income distribution, and no indication at that stage that the problems to be tackled might be concentrated in pockets *within* cities. Though the intent may have been present, there was not yet any specific reference to the inner cities. The important issues that the Working Party felt needed to be resolved, in the light of the context within which the programme had been announced and of the clues culled from the speech, were: to what extent any devised programme of action would be about immigration and race relations, treating ethnic minorities either as generators of problems or as special need groups; what areas were to be covered by the programme and by what criteria they would be chosen; what the scale of the programme would be and through what financial mechanisms it would operate; and what forms of action or activity it would finance – and, if it were to be projects of some kind, what kind they would be. There were of course many other matters of detail to be settled, but in identifying the above issues as the crucial ones the Working Party had fixed the agenda that in large measure would determine the nature of the outcome.

It was clear in everyone's mind that what they were dealing with was primarily an immigrant issue and an immigrant programme. It was equally clear to some members of the Working Party and the Inter-departmental Committee that, in giving the programme an exclusively immigrant focus, they would be treading a political minefield. The immigrant focus resolved itself around two separate but related points: the political sensitivity of discriminating in favour of immigrant areas (and being seen to be so), either by allocating additional resources to them or even simply by having a programme concerned with them; and avoiding the identification, in 'the public mind', of immigration *with* general urban deprivation. The first concern was explicitly expressed in a Parliamentary Committee brief as: 'the general recognition of the political difficulties of setting up the idea of positive discrimination in favour of immigrant areas, however these might be dressed up as urban areas of general social need' (brief for Parliamentary Committee, May 1968). The potential political difficulties referred to were both party-political (that is, they could damage the minister and his party) and political in the wider sense of being fraught with difficulty and unlikely to follow an easy and consensual path through Parliament. They persuaded officials that, even if the main focus of the programme was 'the immigrant focus', this would have to be disguised. Furthermore, the relationship between general urban deprivation, the needs of immigrants (and immigrant areas) and – in some people's minds – the problems *created* by concentrations of ethnic minorities had to be presentationally constructed to avoid close identification of all these. Though these were real, substantive policy problems, they were treated at this stage only as presentational problems, mainly because of shortage of time. Thus, the Working Party on Immigration and Community Relations felt 'that the social effect of Commonwealth Immigration was an element of social need for the purposes of the Programme but it was important to make it clear that it was a different kind of social need from multiple deprivation' (Working Party on Immigration and Community Relations, Minutes, 7 June 1968).

In the event, the Working Party, in considering 'the immigrant focus' alongside a number of other issues, such as project types and criteria for area selection, was able to incorporate the question of immigrant areas into a broader tapestry within which its conspicuousness, if not its significance, was muted. Concentrations of ethnic minority members was to be but one component of urban deprivation and special social need. 'A substantial degree of immigrant settlement would also be an important factor, though not the only factor, in determining the existence of special social need', was how the first circular expressed it (Home Office, 1968c). Likewise, earlier in the year the Home Secretary, in making his announcement about the programme to the House of Commons, relegated the immigrant issue almost to a passing reference: 'The Government have now completed the first stage of their study of urban areas facing acute social problems in the fields of education, housing and health and welfare. Many of these areas include concentrations of immigrants' (Callaghan, 1968). The House, however had not forgotten where it all began, and the ensuing debate was not about general urban deprivation or even about the Urban Programme; it was about race relations and further restricting immigration of Commonwealth immigrants and aliens.

The attempt to steer a middle course for the programme, however, was largely successful, and to the extent that there was ever 'a public view' of the programme,[10] it was not of a primarily immigrant initiative.

The question of who was to receive assistance under the programme was a more practical one, though it too had its presentational aspects. The first thoughts of both the Working Party and the Inter-departmental Committee revolved around the idea of whole towns or whole urban local authorities – at least, as a starting point. Three existing policies or programmes with a priority area component were examined – Educational Priority Areas (EPA),[11] 'housing priority areas'[12] and 'Section 11 authorities' (see p. 51 above) – and a list of all authorities in receipt of help from one or more of these drawn up. Such a list might form the basis for Urban Programme recipients. The idea was abandoned when it was found that the list contained 80 per cent of all London and county boroughs. Other methods of approach had to be found . It was in fact a census exercise conducted by Birmingham County Borough in response to the need to identify EPA schools that came to the rescue and sowed the seed of the 'black spot' or 'needlepoint' idea in the minds of Working Party members. Small-area data showing the incidence of a number of deprivation factors were plotted on overlay maps, and the picture that emerged as more patterns were superimposed was one of localized concentrations of multiple deprivation. The Working Party pursued the possibility of establishing sets of criteria that, at small-area level, would present a short-list of priority 'black spots' which would be the target of programme funds, but for immediate reasons of shortage of time and a more considered view of the problems of defensibility that explicit criteria would raise, the proposal was shelved and eventually abandoned.

The solution adopted for all but the first phase (where urgency dictated a quick selection of 34 local authorities as (recipients) was to let local authorities decide who should benefit. There would be no designated areas, and therefore no quarrels over who was included and who excluded. Selection there would have to be, of course, but that could be dealt with at a later stage and by different procedures. One longer-term consequence of these decisions, however, was that the Urban Programme would never become as discriminatory as it might. Though the Home Secretary (and the Prime Minister) had urged that the programme resources not be spread so thinly as to produce no effect, the decision to invite *all* authorities to participate (even with subsequent rigorous project selection) was not most conducive to this end. In the longer term, since you cannot continually invite participation and then continually reject it, most authorities had to have something, however small, and this inevitably led to dissipation of funds.

The initial level of funding of the Urban Programme had little long-term significance (unlike the selection of areas and project types) except as a base from which it subsequently expanded. It is worth noting, however, that, at the time of announcement of this forerunner of inner-city policies, there was, as far as we can tell, no conception of how big it was to be. The scale and level of funding were among the unknowns with which the Working Party and the Committee had to cope. They did know, however, that the monies had to come from departmental savings, and it is probably the savings that the Ministry of Health and Social Security, the Department of Education and Science and the Ministry of Housing and Local Government (but not the Home Office) were able to provide at the outset that determined the first figure to emerge of £30 million to be spent over two years. This was subsequently reduced to £22 million over two years, and then the same amount over four years. It was a very small beginning (much smaller than either the Home Secretary or the Prime Minister wanted), but it was subsequently to grow to £51.9 million by 1978/79,[13] the last year in which all authorities were eligible for grant aid, and £31.7 million under circulars 18–21 (1979/80 to 1980/81) under the new Traditional Urban Programme arrangements, (see p. 48 above).

The question remained of how these resources were to be disbursed. Two options presented themselves to the Working Party. The first was to allocate the funds to local authorities through the rate support grant using the needs element formula, for the authorities to spend as they deemed appropriate in their 'areas of special social need'. The second was to disburse the funds as a specific grant for approved items of expenditure or projects in the areas of need. The details, however, represented but the tip of a much greater issue, which was to remain a concern of inner-city policies. For the

Urban Programme it was a question of the extent to which it was a central government or a local government programme. For inner-city policies ever since, it has been a question of the most appropriate kind of relationship between central and local authorities for the effective implementation of inner-city strategies. The Partnership arrangements (Nabarro, 1980) and Urban Development Corporations[14] are more recent attempts to find a satisfactory solution to this problem.

For the Urban Programme in 1968, however, it was a question of whether local authorities should make the running and spend the resources in the manner they thought most appropriate to their own particular local problems, or whether the programme was primarily a central government initiative in which central departments could determine, or at least oversee, where the money was to be spent and what it was to be spent on. The Working Party decided upon a specific grant for centrally approved projects on the grounds that

> such a reweighting [of the rate support grant formula] would give no incentive to local authorities to spend on the preferred type of project, and that as the rate support grant was in aid of all the revenues of the authority and not of any specific item of expenditure, there was no guarantee that any additional grant diverted to authorities whose areas contain districts of special need, would in fact be spent on projects of benefit to such areas. [Home Office, 1968a]

Further, as one member of the Working Party later recalled:

> 'We fairly quickly came to the idea of a specific grant system so that we had a sanction over individual projects. The alternatives would have been to put money into the general rate support grant. I felt strongly that this would not have been the way because of our concept of geographical areas, that is, areas of geographical concentration of need. I would not myself have thought of a general grant which the local authority could spend at its own discretion, not so much because of distrust of

local authorities as because this is not what we had been told to do. We had been told to get a central government programme going. [interview with senior Home Office official, 1974]

Specific grant was not without its difficulties, however; potential opposition from the local authority associations had to be anticipated and new legislation would be required. In the event, neither turned out to be very problematic. The local authority associations were more concerned with the rate at which grant would be paid,[15] and the drafting and passage of the necessary legislation (the Local Government Grants (Social Need) Act 1969) were achieved unusually rapidly. (For greater detail of the passing of the Bill, see Edwards and Batley, 1978, pp. 63–5.)

There remained the matter of what sorts of project the Urban Programme should fund. During the life of the Programme the range of projects has continually broadened (though not in response to a purposive problem-directed strategy for the inner cities), but at the outset the list was much shorter. No one had a clearly formulated view of what urban deprivation was or what the major problems of the inner city were that required remedial action. A precision of problem definition was acutely lacking, and though the Prime Minister's speech had mentioned a wide range of problems there was no means of rationally setting priorities. In the absence of a problem-defined strategy, administrative expedience filled the vacuum.

At the first meeting of the Working Party, departmental representatives provided suggestions for the types of particular initiative that their departments would like to see supported, and this list was to become the foundation of the range of project coverage of the programme. (For the complete list, see Edwards and Batley, 1978, p. 54.) It seems likely that two factors were predominant in determining the composition of these suggestions: individual departments' views about gaps in their existing policy coverage, and, perhaps more important, the emphasis in the Prime Minister's speech on an immigrant focus for the Programme and on provision for children and education. It was, in fact, provision for the under-fives (nursery education, day nurseries, day care and pre-school playgroups) that gained most prominence and became almost the sole concern of the first circular. The reasons for this were various, but foremost among them were the fact that the Department of Education and Science was, in the words of one of the Working Party members 'one of the most responsive takers', that it was felt that 'you can't go far wrong in doing things for young children', and that local authorities' familiarity with establishing nursery provision was conducive to a rapid start for the programme.

The range of projects that has subsequently been funded by the Programme is evident from the analyses of project types given later in this chapter. The arguments for promoting each of these cannot be rehearsed here (See Edwards and Batley, 1978, pp. 134–8, for greater detail), but it is interesting to note two ideas that were canvassed but subsequently rejected. Housing provision, initially seen by Working Party members as an important component in the alleviation of urban deprivation, was rejected on the grounds of cost (it would have swallowed the total Programme funds to no visible effect), while the possibility of paying higher rates of benefit to residents of deprived areas was quickly rejected on the grounds of complexity and impracticability.[16] Had such a procedure been adopted, it would have thrown into stark relief some of the moral problems that remain unresolved in relation to positive discrimination, not least the question of what constituted the 'relevant differences' that justify the over riding of the *suum cuique* rule that occurs with positive discrimination (see Feinberg, 1973; Goldman, 1979; Cohen, Nagel and Scanlon, 1977 (especially the essays by Nagel and Goldman); and Behn and Peters, 1959).

It is a measure of our changed perception of the problems of the inner city (probably more than changes in the problems themselves) that, while today unemployment would probably be at the top of any list of inner-city concerns,[17] it received scant attention in 1968. (It is unlikely that this is due entirely to increases in overall unemployment rates; the differentials in these rates between inner cities and non-inner cities has always been high. The Department of Employment and Productivity was represented on the Working Party, but at this early stage the question of employment was raised only in connection with a request that the Working Party examine the possibilities for a programme of immigrant dispersal.[18] Nothing ever came of this.

This, then, was the manner in which the Urban Programme was constructed. In the two months following the Prime Minister's speech much of the foundation had been laid, so that on 22 July 1968 the Home Secretary was able to make a statement in the House of Commons:'The Government propose to initiate an urban programme to help tackle the social problems of the communities concerned. Action will be required on a number of fronts and the programme must necessarily be a continuing one . . . .' There remained much detail to be finalized, but sufficient progress had been made to issue the first circular to local authorities on 4 October 1968. Such was the government's eagerness that something tangible be seen to happen that this circular inviting bids was issued almost four months before the bill enabling payments of grant received the Royal Assent (on 30 January 1969).

Whether the Programme would have been much different in form had its formulation been carried out at a more leisurely pace, and with wider consultation and more detailed consideration of the problems it was designed to alleviate, remains a matter for conjecture, but some of the longer-term consequences of the way in which it was put together will be considered later in this chapter.

THE URBAN PROGRAMME PROCESS

The programme that was to emerge from all this was in effect a mechanism by which a small part of the rate support grant[19] would be diverted to local authorities and voluntary agencies to spend on projects that, with central government approval, would be established in areas deemed by the local authorities to have 'special social needs' or concentrations of urban deprivation. The significance of this is that the Urban

Programme was to become an expenditure mechanism rather than an inner-city strategy, and it is as such that it should be seen in the longer-term context of the development of policies for urban deprivation.

Briefly, the Programme operated in the following way. Each annual phase of the Programme was initiated by a circular issued by the Home Office – in agreement with other interested departments – inviting local authorities – and through them voluntary organizations – to submit, in some priority order, bids for projects to be established in areas of special social need. Bids would be collated by the Home Office and sent to the relevant central government department for consideration. They would return their lists of approved projects (averaging only about one in seven of submissions) to the Home Office, which would make adjustments for overall 'balance' (as between statutory and voluntary projects, between authorities, capital and revenue and different project types) and inform authorities of which projects had been approved for 75 per cent grant aid. The process has changed little over the years, but the modifications introduced after the move to the DOE are detailed later. (For a more detailed description of the operation of the programme, see Edwards and Batley, 1978, ch. 4.)

The Urban Programme process is not central to the thesis of this chapter, and we must be content with this skeletal outline. It needs to be said, however, that the haste with which the Programme was assembled bequeathed it with a number of operational problems including a lack of inter-departmental cooperation at central government level, a continuing ambiguity over the relative influence of central and local government in giving direction to the Programme by determining what sorts of project should be established, and the dilemma for local authorities in being required to submit important and significant projects that they had not already thought up. These and other issues are examined in greater length elsewhere (see Edwards and Batley, 1978, ch. 7).

There were a number of developments in the Programme during the first ten years of its life, but the general pattern remained broadly as outlined above. Its flexibility as a funding

vehicle enabled ministers on occasion to use it to give emphasis to particular aspects of policy, to try out new policy
initiatives, or to give expression to pet enthusiasms. For
example, in 1971 and 1972 additional sums were added to
fund infrastructure works in special development areas, the
DHSS added £1.3 million for the extension of family planning
services and £1.0 million for the promotion of day nursery and
preschool playgroup provision, and another £1.1 million was
injected as additional aid to the voluntary sector promised
(and promoted) by Mr Heath. Notwithstanding these injec-
tions, however, the Programme established in 1968 was to
remain fundamentally unchanged until 1978.

WATERSHED: 1977 AND AFTER

The events that led up to the watershed of inner-city policies in 1977 have been documented elsewhere (Hambleton,
1981; Lawless, 1977; McKay and Cox, 1979; Lawless, 1981;
and elsewhere in the present volume), and we need dwell on
them here only in so far as they affect the story of the Urban
Programme. The chronicle of the events begins in 1972, when
Peter Walker, as Secretary of State for the Environment, set
up the three Inner Area Studies in Lambeth, Liverpool and
Birmingham. This marked the beginning of a closer involvement of the DOE in inner-city affairs. A number of working
papers and reports were published in the next four years, the
final reports were presented in 1977 (DOE, 1977 a,b,c), and the
summary of the reports in the same year (DOE, 1977d). Meanwhile, a Labour government had come to power in 1974 and in
September 1976 Mr Peter Shore replaced Mr Anthony Cros-
land as Secretary of State at the DOE. Under Mr Shore's
direction, the inner-city problem took a higher priority on the
Department's agenda, and in the same month a Cabinet Committee was established under Mr Shore's chairmanship to look
into inner-city policies. Almost immediately, the new Secretary of State made it clear that a new diagnosis of the
inner-city problem was being made, one that would require a
different form of policy response. The first indication came in

a speech he made in Manchester in the same week that he was made chairman of the Cabinet Committee. The emphasis was on population and job loss from the inner cities and the need to attract more industries back into them to help regenerate their economic infrastructure (Shore, 1976).

The following January, two days after the publication of the Inner Area Studies summary report, there was a lengthy debate in the Commons on urban affairs initiated by Mr Geoffrey Finsberg MP. Mr Guy Barnett, Under Secretary of State for the Environment, replied for the Government. The debate is illuminating, not for any insights into new policy direction, but for the very wide range of concerns expressed by speakers (not all, but most, about what we may loosely call the inner-city problem) (*Hansard*, 1977). There was certainly no consensus about what the inner-city problem consisted of, and certainly no indication that the new diagnosis from the DOE was common ground. The new orthodoxy was not apparent in the views from the constituencies.

The following month, Mr Shore expanded on his Department's thinking in a major policy speech made at the 'Save Our Cities' conference in Bristol (Shore, 1977a). In the course of his speech he proposed the idea of partnership arrangements and emphasized the need to bring major policies and finances (such as the rate support grant) to bear on the inner-city rather than relying on small-scale programmes:

> We cannot rely solely, or even mainly, on extra initiatives such as the Urban Programme or Educational Priority Areas. These provide valuable topping-up, and help to ameliorate problems. But if we are to get to grips with the underlying economic and social forces, we must deploy the major instruments of public policy. [Shore, 1977a]

This was the first public and explicit acknowledgement of the inadequacy of the Urban Programme by a government minister, and it signalled the important changes that were to be announced within the next few months. On 6 April 1977, the day after announcing a cut-back in new town policies, Mr Short outlined the government's new strategy for the inner cities (Shore, 1977b). Among other things, responsibility for the Urban Programme was to be transferred from the Home Office to the DOE, 'partnership' arrangements were to be offered to five authorities, and the Urban Programme was to be re-cast and expanded from £30 million to £125 million per year with the intention of a continuing commitment of £1,000 million over the next decade. The strategy briefly revealed on 6 April was explained at greater length in the White Paper published in June. (DOE, 1977e).

The thrust of this paper was of course that inner-city policies had been piecemeal and thus less effective than they might have been, and that what was planned was 'concerted action' and a 'unified' and 'coordinated approach'. It has been argued elsewhere (Edwards and Batley, 1978, pp. 244–5) that coordination can easily become a substitute for effective action, and ought to be secondary to a better and more rigorous formulation of the problems to be dealt with. Nothing that has happened since 1977 gives cause to review that argument. Coordination is an administrative opiate. So long as there are coordinative machinery and inter-departmental forums for discussion, all else will come right. All too often, the corporate approach and coordinative machinery serve no other purpose than to cloak an absence of effective problem-directed strategy. What this meant in practice was that an urban programme was to become *the* Urban Programme. To balance the increase in resources, it would now cover industrial, environmental and recreational provision in addition to social projects, and the increased resources were to be concentrated on fewer authorities arranged in a 'league table', from Partnership to Programme to designated districts and then all others. The major part of total Urban Programme funds was to be allocated to Partnership and Programme authorities and the residue used for the remainder.[20] Designated authorities could also submit projects for non-industrial purposes under the Traditional Urban Programme.

The first Urban Programme circular to be issued by the DOE was dated 30 November 1977 and invited bids for phase 17 of the programme (DOE, 1977f). At this stage the separation of authorities into tiers or divisions had not been completed, and this DOE circular therefore simply continued the Programme in the form it had taken for 16 phases under the Home Office. The new tiered arrangements (and thus the 'new' Traditional Urban Programme) came into effect in early 1978, and the first Traditional Urban Programme phase (though continuing the original numbering sequence) was initiated in August of that year (DOE, 1978b). The monies to be disbursed in this phase, calculated as that amount required to carry the Programme forward at a 'reasonable level', represented, at £6 million, an increase on all previous phases.

Soon after the Conservative Government came to power in May 1979, a period of reappraisal of inner-city policies began. On 14 September 1979 Mr Heseltine, the Secretary of State for the Environment, announced a review of overall policy which included a review of the Traditional Urban Programme. This review was completed by March 1980, a consultative document was published in that month, and on 2 April, in a Written Answer, Mr Tom King, Minister for Local Government, noted that possible future options for the Programme included recasting, or even ending, it (King, 1980).

On 19 August 1980 he announced that the Traditional Urban Programme would be continued, and on 9 February 1981 a further statement was made in the House by Mr Heseltine (Heseltine, 1981) to the effect that the Partnership and Programme arrangements would also continue, though with some procedural simplifications.

We have briefly sketched the course of events from the watershed of 1977 in order to present the context within which the Traditional Urban Programme now operates. We must now go back and look at the programme in more detail over this period, to see how it was affected by – and affected – the emergence of a new orthodoxy about the nature of inner-city problems and the best ways in which they should be tackled.

TRANSITION AND THE NEW TRADITIONAL URBAN PROGRAMME

After the 1977 restructuring of inner-city policies, what was left of the Urban Programme (which became the Traditional

Urban Programme) became very much of a residual item in the overall strategy. We must ask, then, why the Traditional Urban Programme survived at all. Would it not have made more sense to concentrate *all* the available resources on the worst areas? Though serious consideration was given to scrapping the Traditional Programme, it was decided on political (and partly presentational) grounds that, since Partnership and Programme initiatives were *so* specific, a wider component to inner-city strategy was also required. The highly selective nature of Partnership and Programme arrangements would, it was felt, be more defensible if there remained a residual but more widely spread component. In addition, though this is not a reason in itself for continuing new approvals, the Programme had, since its inception, incurred high historic costs in the form of committed grant payments on approved projects. Some level of expenditure would have to be maintained to meet these costs.

Another factor in favour of continuation of the Programme was the support it had had (and continued to have) from local authorities (through local authority associations) and voluntary agencies.[21] The first evaluation of the Programme had evinced this support,[22] and it was a feature also of the second evaluation (or review) undertaken by the DOE (1980b). Not only had the Association of District Councils and the Association of Metropolitan Authorities supported continuation, but also, feedback from local authorities during the review of the Programme clearly indicated that they found it very useful for a number of reasons. First, at a time of public expenditure retrenchment (that goes back long before May 1979), the Programme provided a welcome supplement for useful works that might be only marginally feasible on financial grounds. Second, and most importantly (and here, the local authority view was supported by voluntary agencies), the Programme was seen as an important lifeline for the voluntary sector. The Programme had become the main (and, for many, the only) source of central government funding for voluntary agencies, and on the government side the stated support of the Conservative Government for voluntary initiative argued against cutting this link. Third, the Programme was seen as a useful facilitator of cooperation between the statutory and voluntary sectors, in which role its efficacy went far beyond the simple allocation of funds. And finally, but more speculatively, there may have been the belief (not only, but in policy terms crucially, among politicians and civil servants) that small pockets of deprivation remained to be tackled in areas outside those deemed to have the worst problems. Thus, the 'needlepoint' or 'black spot' conception of deprivation, so important in the original formulation of the Programme, may have been functional in securing its continuation if only as a residual measure.[23] If this is true, it is worth emphasizing that the isolated 'needlepoint' conception of urban deprivation, which in 1968 was strong enough to bear the weight of total government inner-city initiative, had ten years later become so weakened, as to be able to bear only the residual part of the strategy. The major part of the strategy (Partnerships and Programmes) was now predicated on a conception of urban deprivation that saw it as an inherent part of urban economic structure.

PRESENT ADMINISTRATIVE STRUCTURE AND PROCESS

There is no 'organic' relationship between the Traditional Urban Programme and the Partnership and Programme arrangements, but the funding source is the same and the Traditional Programme must carve its slice from the same cake that feeds the others. Of course, given that all local authorities could be placed on a continuum of deprivation (as measured by social indicators), the division of the overall 'inner-city' strategy into a number of programmes should allow for one part to take over where another leaves off. If we assume the most deprived authorities benefit from Partnership and Programme arrangements, then it is likely that the 'next worst' on the continuum will be among the most likely beneficiaries of the Traditional Urban Programme.

The allocation of funds between the various components of the total Urban Programme is proposed by officials in Inner

Cities Directorate (ICD 2) in the DOE and sent for approval by ministers. It begins with the total allocation from the Public Expenditure Survey Committee (PESC) for the package of inner-city policies. (For an explanation of the PESC see Heclo and Wildavsky, 1974.) As far as the Traditional Urban Programme is concerned, the minimum amount of this total that it can take is determined by the level of commitment to non-time-expired projects. Over and above this, a further amount must be voted for new projects at a level that is at least sufficient 'to keep the [programme] credible' (ICD2 official, DOE). In what is then 'an iterative process' (DOE official), a balance of allocation is struck that takes account of the actual and presentational demands of the Partnerships and Programmes – by far the largest consumers of the total.

The process of allocating the Traditional Urban Programme slice of the total funds then follows a pattern that does not differ greatly from that operated by the Home Office since its inception. There are, however, one or two changes of 'style' that require mention and that possibly reflect a greater commitment to the Programme than was the case in the Home Office, where it was marginal to the main departmental concerns.

Some effort is now made (as it was not before 1978, except on an intuitive basis) to balance the allocation of funds with the degree of deprivation in an authority as measured by a number of indicators (applicable at local authority level) derived from the census, the National Dwelling and Housing Survey and other sources. This raised the question of how interventionist the DOE should be in cases where the indicators suggest that a particular authority has a relatively high level of deprivation (that is, relative to other non-Partnership and Programme authorities), but has submitted, either for itself or on behalf of voluntary organizations, insufficient projects to allow a level of approval corresponding with its level of deprivation. Thus far, the DOE has adopted a non-intrusive attitude, which is perhaps inevitable so long as the Programme puts the onus and initiative on local authorities and voluntary organizations.

Second, there appears to be a greater degree of ministerial

involvement in the Programme under the present responsible minister (Lord Bellwin), stemming at least in part from ministerial sensitivity over the types of project funded under the Programme and from a measure of scepticism (probably more so than under the Labour administration) about the worth of some types of project and the motives of some voluntary organizations. This expressed itself in particular in relation to 'political' type projects or organizations that might use, or have used, Programme funds for 'political' purposes,[24] What constitutes 'political' in this context is, of course, a political judgement.

PROJECTS

At the time of writing, the Urban Programme consists of 4,910 projects,[25] which represent the tangible expression of the exercise. The range of types of project is very broad, as can be seen from table 1. The extreme variety expresses, perhaps more than anything else, the absence of any strategy for the Programme and, indeed, any coherent view of what it was that the Programme was supposed to be doing. A conception of urban deprivation that encompasses such responses as 'Provision of Vasectomy Facilities' (phase 7, Bristol, £2,000), 'Nursery Unit at Bulford Army Camp' (phase 7, Wiltshire, £10,271), 'Translation of Department of the Environment Pamphlets' (phase 20, Luton, £500), 'Environmental Improvements to Alexandra Gardens' (phase 18, Haringey, £30,000), 'Development of Terminal Care Service' (phase 7, Portsmouth, £5,040) and 'Contact Tracer for VD' (phase 7, Warley, £900) must be broad beyond meaning. It is fair to say, however, that esoteric schemes that should never have been funded are a minority (though a significant minority). The more general profile of projects funded to date and shown in table 1 gives the distribution of funds and projects over 25 different categories of project.[26] Table 2 presents the same data for a condensed grouping of project types.

Nursery education projects have taken the largest single share of funds of any one project type (12.2 per cent) and have

TABLE 1
NUMBERS OF PROJECTS AND APPROVED FUNDS,
BY TYPE OF PROJECT
England, phases 1–21 excluding holiday projects

Project Type*	Number	%	Funds (£)	%
1	347	7.1	1,738,295	2.2
2	52	1.1	1,719,062	2.2
3	287	5.8	9,155,066	11.5
4	601	12.2	9,695,360	12.2
5	224	4.6	3,021,349	3.8
6	241	4.9	2,421,390	3.0
7	220	4.5	3,745,437	4.7
8	160	3.3	2,089,876	2.6
9	128	2.6	384,695	0.5
10	105	2.1	1,999,648	2.5
11	28	0.6	271,868	0.3
12	47	1.0	343,801	0.4
13	26	0.5	757,982	1.0
14	127	2.6	1,217,999	1.5
15	107	2.2	1,293,132	1.6
16	276	5.6	8,453,118	10.6
17	109	2.2	554,215	0.7
18	309	6.3	6,238,315	7.8
19	77	1.6	649,555	0.8
20	176	3.6	3,919,322	4.9
21	183	3.7	1,083,207	1.4
22	309	6.3	3,931,181	4.9
23	403	8.2	5,213,063	6.6
24	124	2.5	1,909,741	2.4
25	244	5.0	7,667,839	9.6
Total	4,910	100	79,474,516	100

* See p. 71 for details of project types

TABLE 2
NUMBERS OF PROJECTS AND APPROVED FUNDS,
BY TYPE OF PROJECT (CONDENSED)
England, phases 1–21 excluding holiday projects

Project Type (Condensed)	Number	%	Funds (£)	%
1	1,752	35.7	27,750,522	34.9
2	380	7.7	5,835,313	7.3
3	440	9.0	5,884,430	7.4
4	771	15.7	15,895,203	20.0
5	831	16.9	11,426,821	14.4
6	492	10.0	5,014,388	6.3
7	244	5.0	7,667,839	9.6
Total	4,910	100	79,474,516	100

Notes

A   Project Types

1 Preschool playgroups
2 Children's homes
3 Day nurseries and day care
4 Nursery education
5 Adventure playgrounds
6 Other play facilities
7 Youth activities
8 Provision for the elderly
9 Family planning
10 Family advice centres
11 Neighbourhood advice centres
12 Citizens Advice Bureaux
13 Legal advice centres
14 Housing advice centres
15 Other advice centres
16 Community centres
17 Community workers
18 General community projects
19 Volunteer bureaux
20 Accommodation for the homeless and sheltered accommodation
21 Language projects
22 Compensatory education
23 General social work
24 General health
25 Miscellaneous

Notes continued on p. 72

Notes to Table 2 (continued)

B Project Types Condensed

The condensed list of project types consists of groups of the specific types (list A):

1 Provision for children (types 1–6)
2 Other age-group projects (types 7, 8)
3 Advice and information (types 10–15)
4 Community projects (types 16–19)
5 Social work, welfare and health (types 9, 20, 23, 24)
6 Special education (types 21, 22)
7 Miscellaneous (types 25)

---

been the most frequently approved (12.2 per cent). In terms of numbers of projects approved, nursery education is followed by general social work (8.2 per cent), pre-school playgroups (7.1 per cent) and general community projects and compensatory education (6.3 per cent each). In terms of funding, the order is slightly different, with day nurseries and day care taking the next largest share after nursery education (11.5 per cent of funds), followed by community centres (10.6 per cent), miscellaneous projects (9.6 per cent), general community projects (7.8 per cent) and general social work projects (6.6 per cent). When we look at the broader classification of projects represented in Table 2, we see that more than a third of all projects have made some form of provision for children (condensed type 1), and these projects have taken 35 per cent of all funds. They are followed (in terms of numbers of projects) by social work, health and welfare (16.9 per cent) and community projects (15.7 per cent), and in terms of funds these two types are reversed in order. The relatively high proportion of funds (nearly 10 per cent) that has gone to projects of a 'miscellaneous' type is partly a reflection of the fact that the project typology, initially drawn up in 1973, less adequately distinguishes the recent distributions, and partly of the fact that many projects that have perforce been allocated to the miscellaneous category (recent economic and industrial projects that did not exist when the typology was constructed) are high-cost projects. We shall be concerned later to examine some of the changes in the types of projects approved that have occurred since the programme moved to the DOE.

ASSESSMENT

We can now begin to assess the Urban Programme and its place in the development of thinking about the nature of the inner-city problem and of appropriate policy responses to it. We have seen how the Programme came into being and the forces at work that produced it. It began as a hurried policy response to a potentially inflammatory race relations situation and was, in a disguised form, to be a means of injecting additional resources into areas of high ethnic minority concentration. There was a real dilemma for politicians (and civil servants) in the presentational form that the Programme was to take, however. On the one hand, it *was* a response designed to show a positive governmental attitude to ethnic minorities, but on the other, there was the fear of adverse public reaction to a policy specifically designed to favour immigrants and to discriminate positively in their favour in the allocation of resources. The doubts (in the minds of ministers and officials) that this dilemma provoked about the extent to which the Programme should be, and should be seen to be, an immigrant programme were to produce a long-lasting ambiguity about the true nature of the Programme, both presentationally and in its practical administration. Added to this, the hurried way in which the Programme was put together meant that the determining factors of its structure and process were largely administrative convenience and feasibility. There was no attempt to analyse in detail what sorts of problems it was aimed at, and which ones were likely to respond to an injection of assistance, given the nature and size of the resources available. Nor was there any attempt to devise for the Programme a strategy that was causally or sensibly connected with any definable aspect of the wide range of problems that collectively we call 'urban deprivation'. This credibility gap is well illustrated when we compare the description of the areas that should be prime recipients of Programme funds, as given in Programme circulars, with the types of project that have been funded in these areas. The first circular, issued on 4 October 1968, described 'target' areas in terms of 'notable deficiencies in the physical environment, particularly in housing; overcrowding of houses; family sizes above the average; persistent unemployment; a high proportion of children in trouble or in need of care . . .' (Home Office, 1968c). Eleven years later, the twentieth circular stated:

> Evidence of 'special social need' for the purposes of this circular covers: poverty, high levels of unemployment, overcrowding, lack of basic household amenities, old and delapidated housing, educational disadvantage, inadequate community services, severe pressure on the social services, or a poor quality of environment. [DOE, 1979]

Against this picture of deprivation we must note that 40 per cent of all projects to date (phases 1 (1968) to 21 (1981–82)) have made provision for children (nursery classes, day care, etc.), 7 per cent for teenagers and the elderly (youth clubs, old people's day centres, etc.), 8.5 per cent for advice and information centres, 14.5 per cent for community projects (community centres, etc.), 14 per cent for social work and health projects, 11 per cent for special education and 5 per cent for miscellaneous projects.[27] Notwithstanding the fact that – as we shall see – recent years have produced more projects concerned with employment, job training and creation and economic regeneration, the evidence is that the Programme has signally failed to make a connection between the problems it posits and the solutions it provides. Once it settled into the pattern described on pp. 51–60 above it became fossilized, and no real attempt was made to rescue from the piecemeal components a coherent strategy. It remained fundamentally a fund-dispensing mechanism that could not, in truth, deserve the designation 'programme'.[28]

In characterizing the Programme in these terms, we see that contribution to a body of knowledge about, and experience in dealing with, inner-city problems was never a part of its purpose. This was an *ad hoc* response to a particular problem, not part of a learning process (as for example were the EPAS and the CDP). Monitoring and evaluation were never built into the Programme, and though there have been two evaluations over the years, both have had considerable limitations. The first of these[29] recognized the impossibility of a rigorous assessment of the Programme in terms of degree of success or failure in the absence of any clearly stated or measurable goals. There was simply no way of saying that the Programme was reducing urban deprivation, since no clear definition of what this consisted of had been constructed. And the projects that had been funded would have required the benefit of a wide range of specific but different expertises. Furthermore, by far the largest proportion of projects that had been funded (to a greater extent in 1972 when the evaluation began than now) represented some form of provision for children. How were these to be evaluated, and by what criteria and over what time span? Presumably the measures of success would have been the extent to which inner-city children, *as a result of these projects*, achieved better educational qualifications, got better jobs, gained higher skills, earned higher wages, had more secure jobs and committed fewer crimes than they otherwise would have done – and all this 10 to 15 years after the projects were put into operation. Neither the structure of social science research nor the patience of policy-makers nor the lives of governments is geared to this sort of time span.

As far as it is possible to judge, the report of this evaluation had no effect whatsoever in the Home Office, whose response was exclusively in terms of the censorship required before allowing publication. Within the DOE the published version was read by the researcher responsible for the second evaluation and may have been useful in/her conducting it. Certainly, some of the data from the first evaluation were used in the second. In policy terms, however, the effects of this first evaluation were less than negligible.

The second evaluation was an exercise internal to the DOE (DOE 1980b), and had direct policy effects. In addition to giving a general review of the programme and a collation of views about it from officers and project operatives in nine authorities with approvals under phase 17 (DOE, 1980b, paras 3.1–3.17), the evaluation also attempted an assessment of performance of 54 projects approved under phase 17 (in the same nine authorities). It is this part of the evaluation that appears to have had the most specific policy effects.[30] Perhaps the most direct policy consequence was, on the basis of the review's findings, to give additional emphasis to voluntary sector projects: 'The review demonstrated that the projects which fulfil the aims of the programme most closely tended to be voluntary sector projects generally . . .' (DOE, 1980a). The review had attempted to evaluate the projects against seven criteria:

1   they ameliorated a special social need;
2   they operated in a deprived area;
3   they did something that could not be funded from main programmes (this was subsequently rejected on the grounds of difficulty of definition);
4   they were innovative;
5   they encouraged community initiative;
6   they tackled a problem requiring coordination between agencies;
7   they assisted ethnic minorities.

The first two criteria were deemed to be 'fundamental to the Programme' and 3–7 to be 'desirable'. Assessment of projects against these criteria was carried out by researchers who visited the project areas and made (what must inevitably have been) subjective judgements.[31] It was found that voluntary sector projects were more likely to be 'successful' according to all but the second criterion and, that 84 per cent and 90 per cent of all projects were 'successful' according to criteria 1 and 2 respectively. Success rates for the other five criteria ranged from 54 to 22 per cent. The purpose of the exercise was to 'assess the extent to which projects met the criteria laid out in the various Urban Programme circulars' (DOE, 1980b). It is not easy to see, however, that all the criteria chosen are in fact criteria of success. The first two in particular ought to be criteria of *qualification* for funding, to the extent that any project that was not 'ameliorating a special social need' or 'operating in a deprived area' ought not to have been funded in the first place. That a project operates in a deprived area is hardly a mark of success, and what is important in respect of the first criterion is the *extent* to which a project is meeting a need. Strictly speaking, this was an assessment of the extent to which projects met Programme circular criteria rather than an evaluation of success; but it is significant – and this is the main point – that in the course of translation into policy (as represented in para. 2 of circular 21, DOE, 1980a), an assessment of criteria has become a measure of the extent to which projects 'fulfil the aims' of the programme. Even more so is this the case with the other observations in the circular, for example that, apart from voluntary projects, 'projects which straddled service agency boundaries, or operated where main programmes scarcely exist, and projects devising more cost-effective approaches than those normally adopted are also particulary appropriate to the programme' (DOE, 1980a). The wording is ambiguous; 'appropriate to' need mean nothing more than that these are criteria for or characteristics of Programme funding. If, however (as we must assume), it means that projects with these characteristics are more *successful*, then the assertion in the circular that the review provided evidence for this simply is not true – at least, as far as the published consultative document is concerned. To be specific, if we take straddling 'service and agency boundaries' to be a reflection of criterion 6 (see above), then only 22 per cent of all projects had met this criterion; if 'operated where main programmes scarcely exist' is a reflection of criterion 3, then no data were produced because of difficulty of definition; and cost effectiveness was not something the review examined: 'The survey was not designed to identify how far various projects provide good value for money' (DOE, 1980b, para. 3.18).

There are two points worthy of emphasis from all this.

First, not only has monitoring and evaluation never been built into the Urban Programme, but the two evaluations that have been conducted have demonstrated (either purposely or by default) that it is not, in a strict and useful sense, evaluable – certainly not as a programme.[32] As we shall see, this has had consequences for the ability of the Programme to contribute in a useful way to the development of thought about urban deprivation and policy responses to it. The second point concerns the relationship between evaluation and policy development. The second evaluation did have a policy effect – especially in relation to the emphasis on voluntary agencies – but the review was not able to say that voluntary projects had been more successful, only that they more often met qualifying criteria for funding. And unless there is another, very different, version of the review from that published, the other claims made in the circular on the basis of the review are, on closer inspection, unfounded. One suspects that the review did for the Programme what the Programme does for deprivation: both are part of the web of symbolic politics.

We turn now to look at the part the Urban Programme has played in the shifting orthodoxies of the nature and causes of urban deprivation and the appropriate policy responses that have occurred since 1976. In doing this we need to be aware of two separate but interlocking and reinforcing sets of events. The first is the emergence of the 'structural' or 'economic infrastructure' account of urban deprivation (replacing the social pathology account), following the publication of the Inner Area Studies and the experience of the CDP. The second, and later, is the application of the 'new right' philosophy under one of its most enthusiastic promotors – Mr Heseltine – to inner-city policy. We need not document either of these events here – they are examined elsewhere in this book – but we should note the irony that the 'new structuralism' – the emphasis on the decaying economic infrastructure of the inner cities and the need to see the inner cities in a wider social and economic context – promoted so strongly by the Community Development Projects (to the embarrassment of the Home Office), meshed so well with the new Conservative doctrine of economic regeneration. The proposed solutions, of course, were quite different, but the CDP (and Inner Area Studies) diagnosis was one that could be effectively exploited in the promotion of free market, private enterprise solutions.

It is fair to say that the Urban Programme played no part (other than a negative one) in the generation of the 'structural approach', which began to see the light of day in Peter Shore's speeches and was later enshrined in the 1977 White Paper. This document acknowledged the influence of the three Inner Area Studies, but this is only the most explicit of a number of (more implicit) influences. The mood had been developing over a number of years in the writings of social scientists (Rex and Moore, 1967; Harvey, 1973; Pahl, 1970), and since 1974 the Community Development Project had been producing critiques of existing inner-city policies, some, but by no means all, from a neo-Marxist viewpoint. It may well be (but this is conjecture) that, had the prevailing mood in the academic and planning community been different, the Inner Area Studies would have produced diagnoses of the causes of deprivation in Lambeth, Small Heath and Liverpool 8 that were more in line with the earlier social pathology approach, which placed the policy emphasis on education, welfare and health. Had the three studies been carried out ten years earlier, their diagnosis would almost certainly have been different (but not because the problems were much different). Whether this represents development or change we shall examine later. Explicitly, then, while the Inner Area Studies had the most public influence on the post–1977 strategy there were other, wider but implicit, influences. In a sense, the Urban Programme remained aloof from all this, only a fossilized reminder of the old orthodoxy and the Home Office's concern to show an 'acceptable face' to immigration. Its lack of contribution to the changes of thought that were occurring is witness to its failure ever to become anything more than a money-dispensing mechanism. It was its flexibility in this role, however, that enabled it to be put to use in the service of the new orthodoxy, and it is to this that we must turn. We can demonstrate the effects on the Urban Programme of the new approaches of 1977–79 and 1979 onwards, and the ways in which it was adapted to reflect these approaches, by examining the changes of emphasis and types of project promoted in the circulars and the changes in the types of project approved from 1977 onwards.

It is not possible to judge with any degree of accuracy the extent to which particular projects have an 'immigrant' or 'ethnic minority' focus. Some, such as immigrant language classes or grants to ethnic minority voluntary organizations, fall clearly into that category, but many more, with no explicit relation to minority groups, will be located in areas of high immigrant concentration and, either directly or indirectly, will serve minority groups. An assessment of immigrant-related projects based solely on those with an explicit connection would be a gross underestimate of the extent to which the Programme had been aimed at and served minority groups. Some indication of the extent to which the Programme is aimed at such groups, however, is possible from the intentions and hopes expressed in circulars. Notwithstanding the shift in emphasis that took place from 1977 onwards in the conception and approach to inner-city problems, there was little discernable change in the emphasis that the Programme gave to the needs of ethnic minorities, and the current policy of the DOE is to maintain the same balance and emphasis on race relations and ethnic minority projects as when the Programme was the responsibility of the Home Office (information from ICD[2] official, May 1981).

Other aspects of the programme, however, do reflect the changed emphasis of recent years. It is of particular interest in this respect to compare the 'official' diagnosis of the characteristics of urban deprivation with changes in the types of project that have been promoted to alleviate it. While the solutions promoted clearly reflect the move from 'pathology' to structuralism, the diagnosis, because it was always ill defined, has changed little. It is yet further evidence of the credibility gap that has always existed in the Programme between diagnosis and remedy.

In 1976 the sixteenth circular, and the last to be issued by the Home Office, described the evidence of 'social need' (used synonymously with 'urban deprivation') as taking 'many forms: poverty, high levels of unemployment; overcrowding; lack of basic household amenities; old and delapidated housing; educational disadvantage; inadequate community services; severe pressure on the social services; or a poor quality of environment' (Home Office, 1976). Many such areas would contain substantial ethnic minorities. This diagnosis of the characteristics of deprivation has remained virtually unchanged since then,[33] notwithstanding the fact that, during that time, the major areas of deprivation in the country have been taken out of the Traditional Programme and become the responsibility of the Partnership and Programme arrangements. The only concession made to this important change was a brief reference in circular 20 to the need for projects 'designed to relieve small pockets of localized deprivation in urban areas where social conditions are otherwise generally acceptable' (DOE, 1979). That the current diagnosis of the inner-city problem for the purposes of the Programme remain couched in the terms outlined above is difficult to reconcile with the view put by officials of the DOE that there are differences in the conception of inner-city problems between the Partnership and Programme strategies on the one hand and the Traditional Urban Programme on the other. There is an implicit view (according to officials) that in smaller, non - Partnership and non-Programme, authorities, the problems are smaller in scale and finite in character.

As against the relative stability of the diagnosis of the nature of urban deprivation within the Urban Programme during a period when more widely, there had been much rethinking about the problem, the sorts of project that it promoted by way of solution more clearly reflect the vicissitudes of the context. As indicated above, we can identify two main stages to the changes that occurred, and the annual Programme circulars provide convenient benchmarks by which to measure these. If once more we begin with the last Home Office circular (1976) (which, apart from the exhortation to a more comprehensive approach, fairly reflects the pattern of preceding years), we find local authorities and voluntary agencies asked to:

- encourage innovation leading to the adaptation of the main programmes,
- tackle special problems requiring the coordinated

efforts of several local authority departments and/or other agencies, and
– unlock community initiatives.[34]

The first DOE circular (no. 17) repeats these encouragements, promotes, in addition, nursery classes and – the first indication of a change of emphasis – projects that may 'help to ease youth unemployment in inner-city areas'.[35] However, it is because the Urban Programme was not to be the main instrument for implementing the new strategy that this circular so inadequately reflected the outline of the strategy published five months earlier in the White Paper. More of the flavour of the White Paper entered the next circular, however (DOE, 1978b), in which, in addition to the same exhortations as appeared in circular 16, local authorities were informed that applications would be considered for 'grant in aid of environmental, transport and industrial projects' (other than those proposed for districts designated under the Inner Urban Areas Act 1978). That the programme remained, none the less, a mechanism for giving tangible form to whatever was the current concern of ministers or the government, or whatever aspect of social policy it was expeditious to emphasize, is evidenced by para. 9 of the circular, which reminds prospective bidders that 1979 had been designated as the International Year of the Child, and that authorities 'may wish to bear the needs of children particularly in mind and favour schemes which, whilst having the main Urban Programme aims of alleviating special social need, will also help children'. The most recent circular continues this pattern by reminding local authorities that 1981 is the International Year of Disabled People. It is hard to escape the conclusion that, whatever other changes there may have been in the Programme, it remains, as it ever was, the most convenient channel for giving tangible expression to the government's social conscience.

The first shift of emphasis that we wish to identify, therefore, was marked in the Programme largely by the endorsement of environmental, transport and, especially, industrial projects. The second shift – giving expression to the doctrine of the new government – was more clearly marked. The first circular issued under the Conservative Government in 1979 (circular 20; DOE, 1979) again repeats the advice of circulars 16 to 18 but then brings into play, in the pursuit of a solution to the inner-city problem, the government's concern for harnessing the private sector. Thus, the circular informs local authorities that 'The Government is anxious that, wherever possible, funds under this Programme should be used for schemes which will assist in wealth creation rather than consumption; will engage the private sector; and will contribute to making inner cities places where people wish to live and work' (DOE, 1979). And again, 'Projects most likely to be approved are those which involve the private sector, directly or indirectly . . . low cost, value for money schemes reaching out effectively to numbers of disadvantaged people.'

Further expression is given to the same theme in the most recent circular, where priority is given to projects 'involving local firms and business in providing advice, financial backing, or other assistance towards the operation of a project'. In addition, the economic regeneration of the inner cities (a theme common to both the post–1977 thinking and the Conservative Government's attitude to the problem) is given a special place, with £1 million being set aside for projects that are likely to promote such regeneration (other than in authorities designated under the Inner Urban Areas Act).[36]

These changes in the types of projects promoted are reflected in the types of project funded under the programme after 1977, but since central government can only approve what has been submitted by local authorities and voluntary agencies, and since these have not (so far, anyway) fully reflected the changed orthodoxy in the types of submission they make, the shift in the nature of projects on the ground is not as marked as the circular exhortations might lead one to suspect. Table 3 compares the numbers and proportions of projects of different types approved under phases 1–16 with those under phases 17–21[37] (holiday projects are excluded). After 1977, a smaller proportion of projects making provision for children was approved (30.4 per cent as against 38.1 per cent), but these still represent the single most common type of project. A relatively greater proportion were 'community' pro-

TABLE 3
TYPES OF PROJECTS (CONDENSED) APPROVED UNDER
PHASES 1–16 AND 17–21
England

Project Type (Condensed)	Phases 1–16		Phases 17–21	
	No.	%	No.	%
1	1278	38.1	474	30.4
2	261	7.8	119	7.6
3	310	9.3	130	8.3
4	451	13.5	320	20.5
5	608	18.1	223	14.3
6	358	10.7	134	8.6
7	84	2.5	160	10.3
Total	3350	100	1560	100

jects after 1977; and – most significant – projects classified as 'miscellaneous' increased from 2.5 per cent of all projects up to 1977 to 10.3 per cent after that date. Indeed, of all the specific types of project (i.e., the 25 types – see table 2, note A), 'miscellaneous' projects were the most common after 1977 compared with sixteenth in order of proportion up to 1977. As has been explained, since the typology now reflects the range of project types less adequately than in 1973, many more recent projects have been relegated to the 'miscellaneous' category. Predominant among these are the types of project promoted under recent circulars – in particular, environmental works projects, job creation and training projects and economic regeneration or small industry projects (nursery factories, etc.). The increases in these types of project approved over phases 17, 18, 20 and 21 are shown in table 4. The biggest increases in environmental works and small industry projects occurred in phases 20 and 21 under the Conservative administration, while job creation and training projects showed a sharp decline after phase 17, to pick up again dramatically under phase 21.

The preceding sections have attempted to show how the

TABLE 4
ENVIRONMENTAL WORKS, JOB CREATION AND
TRAINING AND SMALL INDUSTRY PROJECTS
APPROVED UNDER PHASES 17, 18, 20, 21
England

Phase	Environmental Works	Job creation and training	Small industry
17	1	11	0
18	15	5	8
20	26	1	20
21	23	23	21
Total	65	40	49

Urban Programme has been put to use in the pursuit of both the post–1977 changed inner-city strategy and the Conservative Government's belief in the effectiveness of the private sector of the economy. While the Programme had virtually no influence on the emergence of the new strategy, it has, notwithstanding its now residual function, been 'bent' to give expression to it. At the same time, it has retained its role as the flexible instrument of the government's social conscience. In respect of the changes that have been wrought in the types of project promoted, the credibility gap between the diagnosis of the inner-city problem that the Programme has always made and the solutions it has proferred has been narrowed. In respect of its 'social conscience' role, the gap is as wide as ever. That the Programme was in essence a money-dispensing mechanism is one reason why it could remain relatively untouched by changing orthodoxies, but a more important reason is that the *implicit* purpose of the Programme, as the means by which successive governments have been able to give tangible expression to their social conscience, has always been more important than its explicit purpose of alleviating urban deprivation.

4

The Lost Years

In July 1974 the Home Secretary, Mr Roy Jenkins, announced
to the House of Commons 'a new strategy for tackling urban
deprivation', the Comprehensive Community Programme
(CCP). Compared with those area policies discussed in other
chapters – the CDP, the Urban Programme and, later, the
Policy for the Inner Cities – the CCP is little known, which is
hardly surprising given its early demise. However, we include
here an account of the Programme, not just for the sake of
chronological comprehensiveness – for it was the major policy
initiative in the period 1973–75 – but more importantly
because the CCP initially represented an ambitious attempt to
tackle urban deprivation: to develop a comprehensive,
Whitehall approach to urban problems, and to involve both
central and local government in a new 'partnership'. The CCP
was therefore very much the forerunner to the inner-city
policy launched in 1977, which is described in chapter 5.

This chapter is, specifically, an account of the rise and fall
of Comprehensive Community Programmes during the period
1974–76, but it is also, more broadly, a review of an attempt
by the Home Office comprehensively to plan policies to tackle
urban deprivation, through the establishment of an Urban
Deprivation Unit, by designating the Home Secretary as the
Cabinet Minister responsible for such urban problems, and by

leading an inter-departmental review of policies in this area. It also aims to shed light on the policy process within central government. In recent years there has been a developing literature on social policy-making. Most of the available case studies deal with policy 'successes', in the sense that they concern policies, like the Open University, family allowances, clean air (Hall *et al.*, 1975) or the Seebohm Reforms (Hall, 1976), that were actually implemented. A study of the CCP is different; it is a study of policy failure. Any attempt to analyse the reasons for this failure involves a consideration of the development of joint planning within Whitehall, the role of the Treasury, relationships between the Home Office and other main spending departments, the role played by ministers and civil servants, the power of Parliament, relations between central and local government, and the secrecy of the government system.

Before reviewing, in some detail, the development of policy, it is important to consider the context in which the Home Office was operating in the early to mid-1970s. The growing concern to develop a comprehensive and coordinated approach to urban deprivation was part of a wider desire to develop a 'joint approach to social policy'. The Cabinet Office 'think tank', the Central Policy Review Staff, led this campaign, and in 1975 issued the report, *A Joint Framework for Social Policies* (HMSO, 1975). Others, however shared this concern. In early 1972 the DHSS, for instance, suggested a 'possible approach to a Joint Social Policy' that would involve the identification of problems of common concern to all Departments, drawing individual departmental policies into relationship with one another and establishing common aims. By 1973 Britain had had experience, albeit on a small scale, of area strategies to tackle problems of deprivation. The Urban Programme had been initiated in 1968, EPAs in 1968 and the CDP in 1969. The CDP had been set up as an action–research programme, and in theory their final reports (which were not expected until the mid-to late 1970s) would have recommended the direction of future policy. However, even in the early 1970s it was clear that new action was required, and the Home Office was neither *able* to wait for the CDP teams' final deliberations, nor *willing* to do so. The political controversies surrounding the CDP (chronicled in chapter 2) had taught senior Home Office officials and ministers one important lesson: *never* do it again.

THE HOME OFFICE AND URBAN PROBLEMS

There were both specific and general reasons why the Home Office was heavily involved in urban policy in the early 1970s. Before the Whitehall reorganization that took place in 1971 following the recommendations of the Seebohm Committee, the Home Office was the department responsible for child care, and, as noted in chapter 2, it was partially this responsibility that had led Derek Morrell to initiate the CDP. This meant that, together with the Urban Programme, the Home Office had policy responsibilities in the urban field. It was also responsible for immigration and race relations, and this was another important factor.[1] However, more generally, it was felt that the Home Office, partly because of its prestige among Whitehall departments – deriving from its long history – and partly because it lacked responsibility for major programmes in areas like income maintenance, housing, education and social security, was in a good position to coordinate government policy across Whitehall. And this theme of coordination was to become an increasingly important one in the coming years. More directly, the Home Office was eager to be the department with 'lead' responsibility for urban problems.

THE URBAN DEPRIVATION UNIT

This chapter focuses on the early years of the Labour Government. However, the story of the CCP starts in the latter period of the Heath Administration. The then Home Secretary, Robert Carr, had been made responsible for coordinating government policy on urban deprivation in June 1973. The Prime Minister had agreed to this at the suggestion of the

Home Office, and on 1 November 1973 the Home Secretary announced the formation of the Urban Deprivation Unit to aid him with his new responsibility. Mr Carr told the House of Commons that 'We must recognize the wide range of problems. It is no good tackling them individually. It is no good bringing housing to one area and education to another. We must have an all-systems approach.' He recognized the need for the government to offer more help to problem areas, the need for more comprehensive coordination of policies, and the need to give extra support to families in deprived areas (*Daily Telegraph*, 3 November 1973). He further announced that he had set in motion 'A wide ranging study of the deeper problems and causes which underlie urban deprivation' (this was the 'PAR', which is discussed later).

Press reaction to the announcement was cautious. Norman Shrapnell, then the *Guardian's* parliamentary correspondent, noted that it was 'A quiet announcement without the smallest fanfare, and this restraint seemed justified. The new organisation is apparently on the smallest imaginable scale, little more than a man and a boy to start with, though Mr Carr hoped it would grow' (*Guardian*, 2 November 1973). *The Times*, in an editorial, said that it was

hard to believe that the steps so far announced will in fact lead to any discernible improvement in the coordination of policies between large government departments jealous of their preserves and careful with their budgets. An action team staffed from the Home Office alone is not likely to exert powerful influence within the Departments of Environment or Education, for example, yet one of the most depressing features of recent policy has been the number of unrelated experiments and pilot studies conducted by different government departments when everyone has been saying that the real task is to achieve the proper mix. . . .[Until there is adequate machinery within Whitehall,] there can be no assurance that a real urban policy will be much more than a gleam in the Home Secretary's eye. ['Help for the Inner Cities', *The Times*, 3 November 1973]

The Urban Deprivation Unit (UDU) consisted, for a brief period, of two sections: one concerned with research under senior economic adviser, Gordon Wasserman, and an action team under Tom Critchley. However, the two sections soon amalgamated under the leadership of Gordon Wasserman, working to Critchley at the Under Secretary level, who also had responsibility for race relations and the voluntary services unit as head of the Community Programmes Department. For most of its life the Unit remained small and consisted of some four or more administrators, one or two civil service economists and three or four other professional advisers ('outsiders' on a short-term contracts), including a social planner, a social statistician and a social policy analyst.[2] The Home Secretary set up a committee to which the Unit would report. Its membership included the Home Secretary, his Minister of State, David Lane, the Permanent Secretary, other senior Home Office officials and officials from the Civil Service Department and the Central Policy Review Staff. This committee did not operate during the period of the Labour government, and, as discussed later, ministerial interest in the Unit was at best irregular and normally absent during most of its life.

THE LABOUR GOVERNMENT

Following the return of the Labour government in February 1974, the role of the Home Secretary as minister responsible for coordinating policy on urban deprivation was confirmed, but not without some initial confusion. After the first general election of 1974, Mr Charles Morris was appointed as Minister of State for 'Urban Affairs'. There was general confusion in Whitehall about this new appointment at the DOE and uncertainty about how it affected the Home Office's role. It appears to have been a mistake, apparently made in ignorance of the Home Secretary's responsibility in this area. (An oft-repeated Whitehall story during these days had Mr Morris telephoning the DOE after his appointment to enquire about what he should do next. The Department expressed total ignorance about his

post. This story is so ludicrous that it is almost certainly false –
or correct!) After a brief flurry of Whitehall minutes, the
Home Office role was reconfirmed, with a slight changing of
emphasis to one of policy development: 'to develop government policy directed to combating urban deprivation'. The
new Minister for Urban Affairs, across the road in Marsham
Street, was given some responsibilities within the DOE – for
area management schemes, for example, and the launching of
a series of 'metropolitan conferences' – but these were
responsibilities of little consequence, and the post was subsequently abolished.

Labour's Home Secretary was Roy Jenkins, and his
appointment seemed to auger well for urban deprivation
policy. His previous spell as Home Secretary had given him a
good reputation in the field of race relations, and some supposed that he might now devote his energy to urban problems.
This was no idle hope, for during 1972, while in Opposition,
he had made a series of speeches that focused, in part, on
problems of poverty and deprivation (Jenkins, 1972). These
speeches showed a concern and idealism that offered hope to
the poorest and weakest members in urban areas. Thus, in one
speech he argued that 'the next Labour Government can be
content with nothing less than the elimination of poverty as a
social problem. It is a formidable but not insurmountable
objective.' In another, he called for an expanded Urban
Programme: 'An eight-fold expansion of the whole
programme would cost only about £120 million per year. This is
not too heavy a price to pay to attack the manifold squalor in
areas where poverty abounds.'

THE HOME OFFICE AND THE DOE

Before reviewing the developments of CCP policy, a point about
departmental responsibilities should be noted concerning the
Home Office and the DOE. As the confusion over Charles
Morris's appointment illustrated, the DOE had a strong interest
in the area of urban deprivation. Apart from mainstream
responsibilities for housing, planning and local government

(and, therefore, closer contact with the local authorities than the Home Office), the DOE had initiated Inner Area Studies, following Peter Walker's 'total approach' philosophy; it was currently developing area management schemes and would soon, under the 1974 Housing Act, introduce 'Priority Neighbourhoods'. It was also interested in the idea of neighbourhood councils. Both the Home Office and the DOE saw their initiatives as relating to urban deprivation, and in advocating them used the same vocabulary: 'comprehensive', 'coordination', 'community', etc. Indeed, in one speech the Housing Minister, Reg Freeson, was to describe 'Priority Neighbourhoods' in very similar terms to the CCP. Referring to a need to relate housing efforts in inner-city areas to a 'total urban approach', he argued that the declaration of Priority Neighbourhoods would 'foreshadow the selection of areas where we can achieve action across the board' (Freeson, 1974).

Even at this early stage, therefore, the Home Office had cause to worry about DOE aspirations in this area, and, while the Home Office maintained 'lead' responsibility in this field for the next two to three years, relations between the two Departments, while often close, were always uneasy.

EARLY THINKING: THE POLICY ANALYSIS AND REVIEW

The early work of the Urban Deprivation Unit (UDU) focused on an inter-departmental review of policy, the Policy Analysis and Review (PAR), on urban deprivation. The PAR approach was a new innovation within Whitehall at this stage (it has since been abandoned) and was designed to bring a fresh and comprehensive look to problems and to consider policy options. The PAR on urban deprivation was set up in 1973 and produced its interim report in June 1974. However, its origins go back to early 1972. A meeting in that year brought together officials from the Treasury, the DOE and the Central Policy Review Staff (CPRS), and the focus of attention at that stage was on planning, housing and transport. However, it was recognized that any study should include social considerations, and hence other departments – DHSS, DES and the Home

Office – would be involved. Towards the end of 1972, however, the social aspects had assumed greater prominence in the minds of officials, and it was proposed that the Home Office should take the lead on the PAR.

The internal Whitehall discussion about the setting up of a PAR on urban deprivation seemed to be influenced more by tactical and departmental considerations than by any recognition that this issue was assuming increasing importance and needed to be tackled urgently. Thus the Home Office, while recognizing that its Urban Programme and a more general, though ill-defined, concern with social questions made the Department suitable for the job, was also concerned that a CPRS-led PAR might call into question the Urban Programme itself. It was also observed that for the Home Office to refuse the lead responsibility would lose it credibility within Whitehall. As for the Treasury, it was clearly influenced by public spending on the Urban Programme (in Treasury terms, a worryingly odd spending programme) and the Treasury wanted this reviewed, in the context of the PAR, before finance for 1975/76 was determined. The Treasury was later to argue that it was not realistic to assume that extra resources were available, and hence the emphasis should be on redistribution within existing budgetary totals. Other parts of Whitehall, too, approached the PAR with their own specific experience, concerns and interests. The DHSS, anxious about existing pressures on health and social services, reserved its position; the DOE was cool and pointed to the burden of the existing housing PARs; the DES was strongly influenced by its experience with EPAs and felt it might be unrealistic to restrict the PAR to urban areas; the Scottish Office had its own experience in this area and was ahead of Whitehall thinking; and the CPRS was anxious that the Home Office should focus on the interaction of major programmes, rather than just on the Urban Programme itself.

By mid-1973, and after a good deal of preliminary discussion – that indicated some of the problems to come in respect of resources and the commitment of other Whitehall departments – the PAR was properly underway with the involvement, at an Assistant Secretary level, of the following departments, in addition to the Home Office: DES, DHSS, the Treasury, DOE, Department of Industry, (DI), Department of Employment (DE), the Welsh Office, the Scottish Office and CPRS.

The aims of the PAR were to examine the whole problem of urban deprivation, the collective objective of Departments in this area, and the best ways of achieving them. At the outset, however, the Home Office approached the task with some caution, seeing the first stage as an exploratory fact-finding exercise which would be unlikely to lead to policy options.

PAR THINKING

The PAR, and the policy recommendations that did emerge from it, was influenced by a number of factors. As part of its work, the Home Office PAR team visited some of the worst areas of urban deprivation in England and Scotland and met with local authorities, voluntary organizations and those working in action projects. They also talked with academics and researchers. The Unit's head visited the United States and met officials associated with America's own 'War on Poverty'. A Canadian himself, he was interested in American ideas and experience. A literature review was also undertaken, and the Unit, through the DOE, initiated a special analysis of Census indicators in order to specify the geographical characteristics of urban deprivation.

There is some evidence to suggest that, initially, some associated with the Review saw the problem in terms of 'social stress', manifesting itself as crime, drug abuse, racial conflict, personal problems and apathy. However, other inputs into the PAR argued that the Review should *not* be just 'a fire-fighting exercise', and instead emphasized more structural causes of deprivation.[3] One particular paper that the PAR team had before them deserves noting, given later developments within CCP thinking. David Donnison, then Director of the Centre for Environmental Studies, had prepared a paper for the UDU and CPRS on the 'Character and Causes of Privation and their Implications for Policy' in May 1973. Among other points, this paper noted that most of the people in deprived areas were *not* deprived, and that most deprived people did *not* live in deprived areas.

Early in its work the PAR team considered what the focus of its study should be, and at the first meeting of the PAR's Steering Committee members considered whether this should be on particular deprived *areas* or – and this was the more widely held view – on deprived *people*. Not only was this an important conceptual question, but the answer to it, in policy terms, would also crucially affect the selection of the Department to take lead responsibility for any new programme initiative that might emerge from the PAR. As noted earlier, the Home Office was aware of its credibility during the preliminary discussions leading up to the Review and such considerations of departmental positioning were probably not absent from the minds of all the officials involved with the Review.

Despite the reservations about the focus on areas, in practice the PAR team quickly developed its thinking towards deprived areas and the possibility of a new area approach in policy. Before the end of 1973 the team was discussing the feasibility of developing a 'comprehensive community programme' and was pursuing questions of finance, the selection of areas, the relationship between special programme grants and main spending programmes, and the kind of administrative structure that would be required in Whitehall for dealing with CCP recommendations. The last was an important question, for the PAR team had been impressed by the criticism from local authorities that there was no one Department in Whitehall with which they could discuss a comprehensive attack on their worst areas (and this at a time when Whitehall was urging upon local authorities the need for corporate management and policy-making). This led to a discussion as to whether a new agency was required within Whitehall, or even outside it.

THE PAR REPORT

The Interim Report from the PAR was produced in June 1974 and was considered by both a committee of Permanent Secretaries and a Cabinet committee before being approved by the Cabinet itself and then being announced in Parliament.

Some features of the Report's analysis can be noted. The Report found that there were 'pockets' of urban deprivation in our towns and cities, and that these contained some of the population's most seriously deprived people. By 'deprived' was meant not only deprivation such as low income, unemployment, mental or physical handicap and so on, but also the poorest physical and enviornmental conditions, the worst-quality services, and sometimes the most insensitive and unsympathetic local government. Furthermore, the PAR reported that the problems faced by the deprived in these areas were deep-seated and complex, and important political and administrative factors militated against their remedy. Consequently, the present range of government programmes, finances and planning arrangements could not tackle urban deprivation: a new strategy was required.

The Report noted that a heavy commitment to financial resources and staff from local authorities was necessary, but that, as resources were limited, positive discrimination in favour of deprived areas was required. In addition, owing to the complexity of the problems, a high level of coordination was necessary between all the various local agencies.

After reviewing various policy options, the Report advocated a strategy to 'forge a new partnership' between residents, local authorities, regional authorities and central government. This could be achieved through a comprehensive community programme. It proposed that a number of the most deprived areas, identified from an analysis of indicators and through discussions with local authorities, should be selected on a 'trial run basis' for CCP treatment. On average they might contain populations of 10,000. Once an area was designated as a CCP area, a special team, established by the local authorities but perhaps funded by central government, would carry out a study to identify the problems of the area and then draw up, in collaboration with Whitehall Departments, regional authorities, voluntary bodies and residents, a set of proposals for action.

The proposals would then be submitted to central government for approval and financial assistance. While the Report recognized that the implementation of the proposals required financial assistance to the local authority, it was not too clear about the question of resources. However, it did estimate that an additional £100 per head of population might be necessary (on average, £1 million for each area), but the implications of this, including the important question of how much money would come from central government, were not considered in the Report. Regarding capital expenditure, it was intended that Departments would accept that the inclusion of a project in the CCP would count as a 'determining factor' in setting priorities for loan sanctions. Furthermore, the Report argued the need for a 'central point' for the processing of CCP projects, which might have, in addition, more general responsibilities for combating urban deprivation. The Report concluded by recommending that, in order to test the idea, a series of trial runs be undertaken, three or four in England and Wales and two in Scotland. The Report floated the suggestion that eventually some 50 CCP areas might be established in England and Wales, with some 40 smaller ones in Scotland.

One crucial phase of the PAR process is the analysis of possible options. In theory, the urban deprivation PAR had fulfilled this requirement, and the Interim Report noted, and briefly discussed, other options before arguing the case for the CCP. These options included raising low income; expanding main programmes; and setting up new agencies. In practice, however, the process was far less rational than this. A number of factors and pressures pointed in the direction of an area approach from the outset, and consequently the Report's analysis of policy options was little more than a charade and a rationale for decisions taken very early in the process.

First and foremost, the Home Office's role as lead Department on urban deprivation was crucial. The Home Office's experience in this area was focused on the area approach, through the CDP and the Urban Programme, and while, as noted already, its experience of the latter was becoming an increasingly unhappy one, it was still wedded to this strategy. Indeed, before the PAR was completed the Home Secretary had agreed to the GLC's setting up two pilot 'deprived area projects' and obtaining grant aid for these – in North Islington and Spitalfields. In part, the Home Office's emphasis on area policies was because this was a strategy that would entail continued Home Office responsibility, whereas some other policy options would not. However, the focus on the area approach also was based on the PAR team's experience of visiting deprived areas. While more scientific evidence might have focused attention away from area policies – or at least placed their potential effect in a broader context – the visual impact of area deprivation in cities like Liverpool and Glasgow was a strong one. Furthermore, Scottish Office ideas made an impact on the Home Office team, as did the experience of projects such as the Liverpool Shelter Neighbourhood Action Project (SNAP). Moreover, public spending constraints favoured 'selective' measures and effectively ruled out more 'universal' options.

Added to these factors was the important consideration of departmental politics. Not only was a Home Office-led PAR likely to advocate a Home Office programme, but, conversely, it was difficult for the Home Office to advocate measures that other Departments – DHSS, DOE or DES – would have to implement. For, while in theory other Departments were represented on the PAR committee to contribute to an overall Whitehall input, in practice departmental representatives were there to protect their own departmental interests, and to make others aware of the constraints upon their programmes.

CABINET APPROVAL

The PAR report was first submitted to a committee of Permanent Secretaries, where it received support, and then was sent to a Cabinet committee chaired by the Home Secretary: the Social Affairs Committee. Again, the memoranda prepared by different government departments reveal the varying perspectives within Whitehall. A DOE memorandum, in the name of Charles Morris, was sceptical: it noted the area management schemes of the DOE; questioned the *small*-areas approach (noting that the inner area of Liverpool had a population of

300,000); and warned against 'creating another element in what is already too fragmented an approach to our urban problems'. DOE officials had warned Morris not to accept any claim on DOE public expenditure programmes until the CCP idea had been developed by worked examples.

The CPRS's perspective on the issue was a broader one, as might be expected. It pointed to the problems involved in the Whitehall handling of CCP proposals from local authorities and raised questions about the implications for departments of accepting the CCP as the central instrument of urban deprivation policy. More importantly, and more informally, the head of CPRS, Lord Rothschild, warned Roy Jenkins about the danger of departmental undermining of the CCP idea. He had in mind, for example, a local authority directing its main housing effort outside a CCP area in response to a DOE circular, or the DES not approving proposals to improve schools in the area. 'Bitter experience' in CPRS over three years had shown the difficulty of getting lasting agreement on priorities between Departments. It was certainly unlikely that Departments would simply fall in line behind the Home Office lead on urban problems. Lord Rothschild warned against going ahead with the CCP *unless* Departments accepted its significance as much more than an additional small-scale programme run by one Department. Privately, he believed that Jenkins should be given an overriding role in regard to urban deprivation.

At the Cabinet committee meeting many of these points were raised and discussed. It was recognized that entrenched departmental interests could act as an obstacle towards coordination and hence to positive discrimination. The important question of adequate financial arrangements with the Treasury was also recognized. The Home Secretary, as chairman summed up by noting some ministerial reservations, but also noted the overwhelming majority in support of the proposals. He said that time was short – and therefore consultation with local authority associations could not take place – as it was politically important for the government to announce practical proposals before any general election.

PUBLIC ANNOUNCEMENT

On 18 July 1974 the Home Secretary unveiled the plans in the House of Commons, which were described in the press release as 'a new strategy for tackling urban deprivation'.
He told the house that the strategy involved:

> the preparation and subsequent implementation by local authorities in collaboration with all those concerned, of a Comprehensive Community Programme containing an analysis of the needs of the areas considered as a whole and proposals for meeting them. These proposals are to be developed through a series of trial runs, and financial arrangements will be discussed with the local authorities.

In the official report it was noted that:

> the aim is to tackle more effectively the problems of those who, in addition to suffering individual household deprivations, such as low income, unemployment, mental or physical hardship, etc., are subject to the poorest physical and environmental conditions and the least satisfactory levels and quality of services.

The announcement then outlined the CCP strategy and concluded by stating that a series of trial runs would take place in four or five areas in England and Wales and two in Scotland.

Although civil service opinion had been against too much publicity for the new plan – concerned that this might arouse expectations among the deprived – political considerations clearly favoured publicity, and at that level the announcement was a success. The *Guardian* announced: 'Labour to give from urban rich to poor', while the *Sun* stated that 'Jenkins plans new deal for the poor'. However, some commentary was more sceptical. For example, the magazine *Community Action* said in an editorial, 'Dab a little CCP on it', that 'the salaried bureaucrats and academics in the Home Office Urban Deprivation Unit have thrown up another smoke screen to hide the real causes of poverty'. They judged the CCP to be 'a con, and a pretty expensive one at that' (*Community Action*, 1974, no. 15). A few months later another community magazine, *West Midlands Grass Roots*, had a cartoon on its front page lampooning the new policy. It showed a mad scientist, representing 'Home Office research', surrounded by test tubes. In his hand he held a new test tube, labelled 'New Formula Comprehensive Community Programme', and the bubble from his mouth observed 'new CCP! . . . this should do the trick . . . a definite improvement on CDP!, (*West Midlands Grass Roots*, 1974).[4]

IMPLEMENTATION

In theory, the CCP had got all the backing it required and was a policy ready to go. In practice the first 12 months were likely to prove crucial. Would the Home Office firm up some of the issues that had been raised, but glossed over, during the PAR and also get the programme moving among the local authorities?

The phase of implementation got off to a good start. In August 1974 the Home Office's Permanent Secretary, Sir Arthur Peterson, proposed the setting up of a new piece of Whitehall machinery, an inter-departmental committee of Under Secretaries 'to develop and coordinate government studies and initiatives concerned with urban deprivation and related fields'. This became a sub-committee of the Social Affairs Committee of the Cabinet; it was known as SAC(U) and was chaired by a Home Office Under Secretary. It first met in October. Among other things, it was to receive regular reports on the progress of the CCP.

Early on in the history of the CCP there was some, albeit fleeting, ministerial involvement, particularly in the selection of areas for CCP projects. This demonstrated a clash between the perceptions and needs of ministers (and senior officials) and those of expert advisers. Not unreasonably, ministers asked for a list of the 'worst' areas in the country. The advisers had to point out that it was not that easy; it all depended on what was meant by 'worst': was one concerned primarily with housing and the physical environment, or with employment prospects, or what? Statistics were available to measure some problems but not others. And while the incidence of problems such as the lack of amenities and over-crowding in small areas (enumeration districts) could be measured, data were not yet at hand to show the proportion of households that suffered from more than one problem. The CCP was all about multiple deprivation, but we knew little about its incidence and location.[5] In practice however, and rightly, selection of trial run areas for CCP projects was not an objective, scientific exercise. Other factors were important: for example, which authorities had good chief executives and a corporate management structure that could implement the CCP (although what would happen in those areas, including some of the worst, that did not have these things?). There was also a need to avoid areas, like Liverpool, that were already up to their ears in special area initiatives.

Eventually six local authorities were chosen and approached: Bradford, Gateshead, Wandsworth, Wirral, Merthyr Tydfil and Motherwell. Immediately, problems began to arise. Local authorities claimed that it was difficult to select the 'worst areas. With the Wirral, for example, there were three equally bad areas; in Wandsworth there were five. The Scottish Office reported that the problems of Glasgow were so severe that the CCP approach was not appropriate. Those in the Urban Deprivation Unit became worried about the feasibility of maintaining that we had a useful tool for tackling urban deprivation if it was not appropriate for the worst areas. Chief executives also queried the difference between the CCP and the Inner Area Studies. And significantly, the chief executives of both Wandsworth and Wirral asked why the CCP was a *small* area approach. They argued that problems of employment and income could not be tackled in this way.

These points produced doubts in the minds of Home Office staff and seriously undermined confidence in the new strategy. The CCP was reformulated. It was now suggested that more than one area could be chosen within each local authority; the 10,000 population standard was not to be a rigid rule; and the possibility of a focus on groups was also noted. However, it remained mainly an area approach, focusing on those suffering from a combination of personal and environmental disadvantage.

The beginnings of a move away from a *small* area strategy were reinforced by the emergence of evidence from Census data, the CDP teams and the Inner Area Studies. All of these implied the need for a non-spatial approach with a focus on main programmes and on questions relating to employment and industrial location. In particular, it was evidence commissioned by the UDU, from the DOE, on Census indicators that was to have the most influence. The DOE's Sally Holtermann explored Census data to examine the spread of deprivation throughout Great Britain. She found that, while there were many areas with high levels of both housing problems and unemployment, 'spatial' coincidence of these problems was far from complete, and further that, although there was some degree of spatial concentration of deprived people into the 'worst' areas, there were large numbers of deprived people who lived outside them (Holtermann, 1975b). These findings heralded the end of an age of innocence within the Home Office about the small-area approach. These facts were seriously to knock off course 'the new strategy' that had barely started to gather speed.

While the reformulation of the CCP at this stage was justified partly on the grounds of this 'new' evidence, it was nevertheless a little difficult to understand. First, the evidence was hardly new, but rather reinforced existing knowledge. Experience of EPAs, for example, had led one of the EPA researchers, Jack Barnes, to note that: 'Area policies can only meet the needs of poor people in poor areas; but most poor people do not live in poor areas; and most of the people in poor areas are not themselves poor' (Barnes, 1974). This had been published in 1974, in a Fabian pamphlet, and this knowledge was available during the PAR exercise. Also, as noted earlier, David Donnison in his paper for the Home Office and the CPRS had made the same point in early 1973. The strength of this 'new' evidence, reinforced by local authority chief officers and other officials, was to lead during 1975 to a further reformulation of the CCP idea. This involved a further move away from a focus on areas and an emphasis instead on main programmes and deprivation in general. There was increased emphasis also on the redistribution of resources; in fact, the move away from small areas gave way to a new interest in regions and regional machinery of government. It is perhaps not wholly surprising that chief executives backed the latest reformulation of the CCP: anxious to consolidate their still uncertain role within local government, they were likely to be backers of strategies that would strengthen their position.

How should this new shift in policy be assessed? The focus on main programmes and deprivation might be seen as a step forward in thinking. And the move away from a small-area focus was not before time. In principle, the reformulation also offered a better chance to tackle structural causes of deprivation, such as unemployment and questions of industrial location. However, in practice this was not the case. It did not lead the Home Office to focus renewed attention on the need for Whitehall cooperation and the positive involvement of major spending Departments. Neither did it lead to a focus on issues of unemployment and industrial location, or to a need to include in the exercise the Departments of Employment and Industry. And it was becoming clearer that there would be no real money available to back up the new CCP approach. The focus now was on what local authorities could do for themselves, in terms of coordination, both between their own departments and with other agencies such as the health authorities; on the need for more efficiency locally; and on deprivation in corporate management. This emphasis was an important one, and it was usefully developed with the help of Birmingham University's Institute of Local Government Studies, whose Professor John Stewart was heavily involved with the Home Office on this programme, and the chief executive of Birmingham Corporation, Mr Amos. However, this relatively narrow focus on corporate management was not what the CCP was originally intended to be all about, and could not deliver the goods in terms of offering a 'new approach' to the problems of urban deprivation.

Doubts about the CCP idea led not only to a lack of confidence within the Home Office, about the programme, and to a vagueness in presenting the idea to others, but also to doubts among local authorities who had been invited to participate. The authorities, usually through their officials, increasingly saw the CCP as a relatively narrow management exercise. The Programme was easy to understand in these terms, although because of this some doubted its overall importance. But the involvement of the authorities in discussion reinforced the narrowness of the perspective. Some local government officers, for example, doubted the relevance of 'community participation' in what was now a management exercise and reinforced a growing Home Office prejudice against this aspect of the Programme.

A year after the Programme had been announced with some enthusiasm in the House of Commons, the CCP had made very little progress. It was a vaguer concept than it had been 12 months previously, and the talks with local authorities and others were dragging on and on. At this stage, in June 1975, ministers started to worry about the Programme. They had not been involved with the exercise for some months, but now they asked questions. They called for some speed in implementation, but were told that local authorities wanted more details before they could make a firm commitment. It was hoped to get trial runs going by the autumn of 1975. It was observed, however, that if public expenditure was cut, it might be difficult to launch the CCP properly. In July the Home Office decided that its ministers could not announce any further progress before the autumn recess of Parliament.[6] Lord Harris, the Minister of State, was *informed* of this decision, rather than having been properly consulted. He was told that an announcement would not now be possible. He was also told about Treasury opposition to additional expenditure and was advised that little would be gained by trying to force the issue immediately.

Lord Harris became disillusioned with the CCP. Treasury opposition suggested to him that further progress was unlikely to be made. He suggested that the Programme be abandoned. This would be a disagreeable course of action and would damage the Department's reputation, but he could not see a serious alternative. In August the Home Secretary became involved in the discussions. He was concerned about the little progress that had been made in implementing a policy agreed over 12 months earlier. When told about the difficulties of developing the CCP idea, for example in relation to the relative lack of concentration of deprivation in small areas, and 'staffing difficulties', the Home Secretary said he understood the difficulties, but nevertheless thought progress had been slow. He wanted results by early October. But by the summer of the following year tangible progress had not been made, and by then the DOE was in the driving seat.[7]

CONCLUSIONS

Why was it that a new policy, which originally was concerned with the broadest possible definition of urban deprivation, and which seemed to offer scope for tackling the problem in a radical way, became, within 12 months of its original formulation, nothing more than a local corporate management strategy, albeit with a focus on deprivation?

The main conclusion from the evidence is that the CCP took the direction it did because that was the easy road. The Home Office, whenever it came up against a serious barrier, instead of confronting it, by passed it. Public expenditure was always likely to be a problem, and the financial atmosphere had worsened steadily during the 12 months after the House of Commons announcement. The Treasury was never likely to be an ally, but its attitude too had steadily worsened. Although relatively small amounts of money were at stake – say, £4 million or so during the first year – the Treasury was opposed to this, and threatened to brief its ministers to this effect. Similarly, it was always going to be a major test of the policy as to whether genuine joint planning between major spending Departments could be achieved. This was a major challenge for the joint approach to social policy being formulated by the government's 'think tank', the CPRS. But the challenge was never faced. Departments said it would be very difficult, and this was accepted. Similarly, although this was never a big issue in practice, the 'community' aspect of the programme became a charade. 'Community' was a good word to have in the title, but it never meant very much, and the Home Office knew all too well, from the earlier CDP, the problems it could bring. Local government officials were none too keen either, and this aspect of the Programme was quietly dropped.

Faced with these problems – the major issues that the CCP was set up to confront – the Home Office's inclination always was to back away. Urban Deprivation Unit Staff were given no encouragement to face up to these issues; instead, an easier path was found. This involved not so much implications for central government, but rather challenges for local government. Should not local authorities think critically about their own programmes and how they matched local needs? Was there not scope for a corporate approach to local problems? Local authorities were urged along this path. It did not really require any new central government money (except a smaller amount to set up a local team), and other government Departments did not have to get thoroughly involved, at least at the early stage. The academics and other experts brought into the confidence of the Urban Deprivation Unit reinforced this strategy. The experts who were consulted were the ones who knew all about local authorities, about issues concerning management and local coordination. Other academics, with interests in employment and low pay, for example, were not so confidentially consulted.

In the introductory chapter we discussed the various, and varying, reasons for the increasing emphasis, since the late 1960s, on area approaches to tackle the problem of urban deprivation. We also noted the controversies surrounding explanations of urban problems and discussed the concept of 'urban deprivation' or 'inner-city problems'. This analysis showed the broad nature of the problems we are discussing and, by implication, the difficulties facing even the most committed government when it comes to tackling these important problems.

'Urban deprivation' and problems of the 'inner city' are in many respects merely labels that are put on packages of social and economic problems. Many of the items in the package remain constant over time (for example, poor housing), but the relative importance of the items varies from year to year, from one locality to the next, and depends crucially on individual, institutional and political perspectives. Observers and policy-makers have different priorities from one another. Occasionally 'new' issues dominate the discussion – in the late 1970s, for example, the state of the economic base of the inner city, or more recently, relations between police and the citizen. By any measure, the items in the packages include some of the most important and intractable problems that are on the agendas of politicians, policy-makers and administrators – unemployment, industrial decline, housing, inequalities within the education system, race relations, and questions about the government system (including relationships between central and local government) and its impact on people (Wicks, 1978).

The CCP approach in particular, and the Home Office's coordinating role during the period 1974–77, is therefore a case study of the attempt by government at that time to grapple with the problems. The conclusions to this case study could be wide-ranging; however, we will focus here on only a few issues, and in particular on the lessons, and insights, from these years for our understanding of the central government system.

The CCP policy can be viewed initially as a bold and brave attempt to tackle the range of problems noted above. Despite the emphasis on coordination that emerged late, much of the thinking behind the CCP in 1974 was based as much on a structural analysis as on a technocratic one, with a strong orientation towards employment and the need to redirect main spending programmes towards the needs of deprived areas. These were the concerns of the professional staff working in the Urban Deprivation Unit at that time and, certainly in the summer of 1974, there was some hope that the CCP might become not just another cosmetic area strategy, but an effective means of combating urban deprivation. Sadly, the CCP story since then is one of dismal failure. In the years that followed, the Programme disintegrated into an area variation of corporate management, implemented at a pace that would embarrass any self-respecting snail, and ultimately running completely into the ground.

How can we explain this failure?

'Urban deprivation' brings together some of the most difficult problems on political agendas. It is complex as a concept, and to tackle it successfully requires clear vision, much commitment, extra expenditure and a toughness and authority within Whitehall. In retrospect, it can be argued that even in the best of circumstances the course would have been a difficult one, and, given the obstacles, relative failure was always the most likely outcome. In practice, however, the CCP never even started to run the course properly and was never given the backing that it deserved.

The performance of the Home Office during these years was paradoxical, with a sharp contrast between a determination to maintain a 'lead' role and a failure to develop that role. We have seen that the Department sought to hang on to its responsibility in this area. It had already lost child care to the DHSS, and there was a general concern within the Department to maintain some non-law and order responsibilities for the sake of departmental status and image. In 1974 it had beaten off an ill thought out attempt to give the DOE strategic responsibilities in this field, and in 1976–77 it gain attempted, this time unsuccessfully, to keep responsibilites at a time when the initiative was moving the DOE's way. Given this eagerness, a determined Home Office, wishing to make sense of its coordinating role in this policy area, might have achieved a breakthrough. But its officials showed no real interest in developing the role of the Urban Deprivation Unit and in getting other Departments to make a genuine effort to help deprived areas. It became clearer and clearer that the Home Office did not view its urban deprivation brief as a priority. Indeed, there was a lack of understanding about the issues, and certainly no sense of urgency.

The inertia of senior Home Office civil servants was sadly compounded by the apathy of Home Office politicians. In his

1972 speeches, Roy Jenkins had called for a 'victory' for Labour at the next election: 'only that will enable us to carry through a programme which will give us pride in our Party and confidence in our processes of government'. The problems of urban deprivation were a major challenge to these processes, yet the history of the CCP during Jenkins's Home Secretaryship did little to restore our pride or our confidence in the Programme. The one minister with real commitment in this area, although no direct responsibility, was Alex Lyon; and he was the one Home Office minister during this time who was sacked. As he observed:

Despite two years of valiant work by experts recruited to the Unit, nothing has been achieved because bureaucratic ineptitude has been compounded by ministerial indifference. It is lamentable that a Labour Government has done so little about an essentially socialist ideal, but it is tragic for the urban deprived – black and white – who continue to suffer. [*Sunday Times*, 26 May 1976]

How do we account for this lack of political interest? This is not an easy question to answer, but a number of factors would appear to be important. The main concerns of the Home Office revolve around other issues, such as police, prisons and, more recently, immigration. To the traditionalist this is what the Home Office is all about, and these issues largely dominate the time and energy of Home Office ministers. Many of the issues have their fair share of crises, and ministers will often act as trouble-shooters at short notice. Compared with this, the field of urban deprivation was a comparatively new one, and had not filtered through Home Office corridors of power as a major concern. The problems of the urban deprived were therefore not the stuff of private office small talk, nor were they, normally, on the minds of senior civil service advisers. In contrast, for example, to the work of the Supplementary Benefits Commission in the late 1970s, which attracted to it some of the DHSS's best officials (Donnison, 1982), Home Office officials seemed to regard the UDU as a backwater from which they sought to escape as soon as possible.

It would also appear, however, that Mr Jenkins himself, whatever he might have said in 1972, was little preoccupied by these issues. His own political future was uncertain – a few years later he was to go to the EEC as President of the Council – and he was thinking through his future steps. It would seem that even at this stage he was discussing with close colleagues, including Lord Harris, the possibility of a new political initiative in Britain. Meanwhile, he was concerned to keep a watchful eye on Mr Benn and those on the left of the Labour Party, and to combat their more socialist initiatives within government. He was in any case disappointed to be back at the Home Office and would have preferred, say, the Foreign Office.

Another major barrier standing in the way of the CCP strategy was the traditional and deeply-rooted departmentalism of central government. The CCP was a brave attempt to focus attention on an issue that cut across Department boundaries and, indeed, to highlight a subject that had implications for much of Whitehall. At least five Departments had programmes or policy responsibilities that directly related to the problems of deprived areas. In practice, it was relatively easy to line up government support for a comprehensive approach during the initial phase of policy development. However, this was partly because no crunch questions were thoroughly worked through. Such questions related to finance (where the money would come from and how the CCP would affect budgetary priorities within departments) and the closely related issue of how the CCP, once drawn up, would be handled within Whitehall. The CPRS had warned in 1974 that, once Whitehall started 'unpacking' the proposed CCP and trying to rearrange the elements to fit the priorities of individual Departments, things would be back where they started.

In practice, it can be argued that the CCP experiment involved a conflict between opposing interests. In one corner were the major spending Departments – DHSS, DOE and DES – and the Treasury, who in practice were antipathetic to any initiative that threatened departmental autonomy. The traditions and conventions of these Departments – their public spending patterns, planning systems, civil service career structure and training – militated either explicitly or implicitly against the joint or comprehensive approach. In the other corner was a weaker grouping and a more motley crew. They had no real traditions to back them up, and certainly no money, but they had ideas and aspirations. They included some of those working within the Urban Deprivation Unit – often 'outsiders' – the CPRS, some ministers (at an early stage David Owen of the DHSS had offered support to the Home Office, and had warned against his own Department's conservatism) and some backbench MPs. In the best possible circumstances this was an uneven battle. In the circumstances of expenditure constraints and politicians' inertia and apathy from within the Home Office, the contest hardly ever took place.

While the failure to break through the departmental mould of Whitehall is a major 'lesson' that emerges from the sorry saga of the CCP, it is hardly a blinding revelation. The problems could have been foreseen at the outset of the CCP; indeed, they were foreseen. As noted earlier, *The Times* had argued in 1973 that there was a need for adequate machinery within Whitehall and, that, until this was created 'there can be no assurance that a real urban policy will be much more than a gleam in the Home Secretary's eye' (*The Times*, 3 November 1973).

The major barriers standing in the way of a successful implementation of area deprivation policies involve some important and complex questions. But the main issues are essentially political. Although urban deprivation policies are often discussed in an apparently neutral language (with much talk of 'coordination', 'consultation' and 'better management'), there is no way in which these more technical questions can be successfully addressed without a commitment to greater equality and social justice. For most of the period of the last Labour government this commitment was missing, and in its absence it was civil servants who did most of the thinking about urban deprivation, who developed the ideas and fashioned new programmes. During the period of 1974–79, there were three major reviews of urban deprivation policy; none was published and only one was publicly announced. Major problems were discussed behind closed doors, although there were many outside Whitehall who could usefully have contributed to such discussions. Even back-bench MPs stood no chance of successfully questioning the Executive about developments. Parliamentary questions were taken seriously, but often answered misleadingly, having been drafted with more regard to the need of the Department than the rights of the House of Commons. More specifically, the early secrecy surrounding the PAR review meant that local authorities were excluded at this crucial stage. As noted, this was to cause problems during the stage when the Home Office attempted to implement its plans.

POSTSCRIPT: REFOCUSING ON INNER CITIES

Coincidentally – for there appears to be no evidence to link the two – at the very time when the CCP had run out of steam, there occurred a political initiative that was, albeit after a false start, to put impetus behind urban deprivation policy. In August 1975 the Cabinet met at Chequers to review public spending. Among the priorities that emerged for safeguarding, as Barbara Castle records in her *Diaries*, were: 'housing (not housing subsidies), industrial retraining, and inner cities' and the emphasis on the inner city came, significantly, from Peter Shore, the Secretary of State for the Environment: 'the only spending priority he would insist on was the inner city areas', noted Barbara Castle, (1980). The view from Chequers that reached Whitehall was that high priority should be given to the problems of the inner city; it was a complex matter; there was a case for setting up a team to consider the whole question; race and inner city problems were not coterminous, but they did overlap; and there might be arguments for greater government corporate management.

The task was entrusted to an inter-departmental group of officials under the chairmanship of the DOE's chief planner, Wilfred Burns. The responsibility appears to have gone to the DOE because of the important role of local authorities, but whatever the reason, it was the first clear sign that the battle between the Home Office and the DOE was moving in favour of Environment. The Home Office was aware of the implications and complained internally that the Burns Committee's brief seemed to have been prepared in total ignorance of the Urban Deprivation Unit's work over two years. It was felt that there was little knowledge of the CCP initiative within senior levels at the DOE. At first, however, there was some satisfaction within the Home Office that the work of the Committee was emphasizing the role of the Urban Programme and the CCP: it was felt that the Home Office's views were being achieved without the need for 'hard in-fighting'.

The Burns Report

The Burns Report, which was never published, defined the inner-city problem in terms of the spatial concentrations of the poor or deprived. It concluded that the main benefit to the inner city would be secured by the progressive adaptation of main programmes. This emphasis was an important one, although it was very much a reiteration of the earlier PAR report. However, it stopped short of proposing any decisive action on this front. Rather, it specifically did *not* propose any transfers between PESC programmes and merely suggested further work that could lead to a case for more expenditure. It did, however, argue that the adaptation of main programmes should be considered by Departments and should be a feature of any new policy reviews.

The Burns Committee recommended the continuation of CCP work and saw this as a means of promoting closer working relationships between central and local government. But this fell far short of enthusiastic backing for the Home Office's 'new strategy'. Similarly, the importance of the Urban Programme was noted, although the Committee recommended that the Programme in England and Wales needed to be redirected and more coordinated with other local initiatives. It was therefore recommended that officials review the Programme. They felt that 'relatively modest' additional sums were necessary.

The Burns Committee ruled out any further examination of new policy instruments such as a new specific grant, new executive agencies, a new government agency, or new area plans from local authorities. Having reviewed statistical data, the Committee produced a list of authorities with 'substantial urban problems' including the 'worst' such problems. The list included eleven London boroughs, nine other English authorities, one area in Wales and nine in Scotland. The Committee felt that such a list could *not* be publicly adopted but could be useful within Whitehall as, *inter alia*, a 'touchstone' of policy.

Despite some useful analysis and suggestions – a recommendation, for example, that there should be a study of inner-city employment problems and possible measures – the Report, while recognizing the problems, was short on decisive recommendations and commitment. Its conclusions spoke of substantial difficulties and felt that any progress would be conditioned by expenditure and manpower constraints and limitations of knowledge. However, it noted that a 'new thrust' of policy was possible if ministers wished it. The ball was back in the political court and, at last, ministers saw it coming.

The Shore Committee

The Home Office was unimpressed by the Burns Report. The Permanent Secretary noted that it contained virtually no new ideas and he proposed instead the creation of a new agency to tackle the problems, with responsibility for such policies as the Urban Programme. Such an agency would be able to provide greater continuity in the development of policy; it would be a focal point for local authorities; and it would be a visible sign of government's concern. The Home Secretary felt that this was an excellent and constructive idea; however, it seems never to have been pressed.

The Cabinet ministerial group on inner-city areas met in August 1976 to discuss the Burns Report. It recognized that when resources were scarce it was very difficult to get agreement to shift resources between programmes. It was felt that for these reasons, and because local authorities might not always wish to allow favourable treatment to inner-city areas, there was a case for suggesting that further ministerial consideration should include the possibility of a more radical approach, which might include switching resources between programmes and more central direction of local authorities.

The Prime Minister summed up the discussion. He reported that he had held a meeting of junior ministers in May and the main point of concern had been that urban policies needed more attention and that responsibility for it was too fragmented. The Prime Minister thought that junior ministers would be enthusiastic to tackle the problem, and they had more time available than senior ministers. Therefore a group of junior ministers should be established under the chairmanship of a Cabinet minister to approach the task in the light of Burns but on a 'no holds barred' basis. They should consider the possibility of selecting two or three areas on the basis of a political judgement in which a concerted effort would be made to solve the problem (on the lines of the Strathclyde project). They should assume no additional resources, but concentrate on reallocation.

The story of the 'Shore Committee' is taken up in the next chapter. Here we need note only that, some three years after the establishment of the inter-departmental review of policy towards urban deprivation and two years after the announcement to the House of Commons of a 'new strategy', events had turned full circle: another review was under way, more thinking was to be called for, options were to be discussed. The inner cities were three years closer to the ugliness of the 1981 summer. The period of Home Office responsibility had been the lost years, for urban policy.

5

Peter Shore and Inner-City Policy: The Last, Best Hope?

> Taking the post-war period as a whole, the most striking thing has been – until only three or four years ago – the failure of public policy to recognize the central fact of the economic decline of the inner city.
> [Peter Shore, Thomas Cubitt Lecture, January 1980]

This chapter considers a late phase of urban policy: one distinguished from those described in earlier chapters by both the scope of the intervention attempted and the scale of the resources devoted to it. The politician most closely associated with it was Peter Shore, Secretary of State for the Environment in the Labour government of 1976–79; and the policy itself is most conveniently labelled 'inner-city policy', from the White Paper in which the rationale for it is set out, *Policy for the Inner Cities* (DOE, 1977e). The singular and plural were clearly intentional: the object was to integrate all the various lines of approach that had been developed in the course of previous experiments and apply them on as wide a canvas as possible.

Indeed, the style in which the White Paper itself was produced as a departure from past practice. A systematic attempt was made to set out policy objectives in advance of a new initiative. This was a sharp break with the previous approach, by which such new initiatives were worked up and their objectives defined, if at all, in the privacy of Whitehall. As a document, the White Paper reflects the flavour of the new initiative – in a nutshell, the search for the most effective administrative solution. But before exploring the exact form and direction that the new initiative and policy took, we should first set it in its political context.

In political terms, the environment for a major new initiative in social policy in 1976 was not at all favourable. The attempts of the Wilson administration, with its narrow majority, to redress by sleight of hand the economic setbacks of the last days of the Heath government – the crumbling away of the Barber boom in the twilight of the three-day week – had collapsed in ignominious failure. Hyperinflation seemed for a giddy moment to be a real possibility. The enforced reductions in public expenditure introduced by Wilson's successor, James Callaghan, as a price of support from the International Monetary Fund had closed the door to any new departure in policy with significant resource implications. Furthermore, the government's unpopularity had reaped the usual sour fruits of mid-term electorial setbacks. By-election defeats had set the government teetering on the brink of disaster, held back only by the uncertain support of the minority parties in the House of Commons. More ominous still, unemployment had risen steadily to the figure, unprecedented since 1945, of 1.4 million. The problem of the rapid decline of inner-city employment, even in the more prosperous conurbations, and with it the possibility that jobs, both skilled and unskilled, in manufacturing industry would be permanently lost had finally come into focus for politicians and planners alike. By 1976 the pace of decline in London's industry had become so great that the GLC was forced to re-examine one of the key objectives of postwar planning in the South-east: the positive encouragement of movement out from London of people and jobs to the new and expanding towns.

Finally, the half-stifled issue of race relations was also emerging into the open. The anxiety of the Labour government had been sharpened by the evidence of unrest in several areas of ethnic minority concentration, and worst of all by the activities of the National Front, which had made ominous progress at local government elections. In the summer of 1976, therefore, Labour Party tacticians decided that 'a major new campaign against racialism' should be launched. A joint meeting of the Party's Organization, Publicity and Home Policy Committee authorized the initiation of a major publicity campaign to start in September 1976 with leaflets, ministerial speeches, and meetings (*Observer*, 18 July 1976).

While these political and economic pressures were mounting, evidence from the earlier initiatives in the field of urban deprivation was beginning to accumulate in Whitehall. Of these, the most striking was the account provided by the Community Development Project (CDP) teams, who produced in *Gilding the Ghetto* a highly coloured version of the origins of the Urban Programme and the objectives that it had served. On the cover, a photograph of a smiling James Callaghan strode confidently away from a background of urban decay. Without necessarily endorsing the Punch and Judy version of past events provided by the CDP teams, a good many other commentators had become impatient of the small-area approach which still formed the major element in the government's programmes. In his Barnett Shine Foundation Lecture, Peter Townsend commented that,

> however economically or socially deprived areas are defined, unless nearly half the areas in the country are included there will be more poor persons or poor children living outside them than in them. There is a second conclusion. Within all or nearly all defined priority areas there will be more persons who are not deprived than are deprived. Therefore, positive discrimination based on ecology will miss out more of the poor and deprived than it will include. It will also devote resources within the areas predominantly to people (or children) who are not poor or deprived.

From this he drew the conclusion that

> it is the national structure of unequal resource allocation on the one hand, and the sponsorship of styles of living

on the other, mediated by social classes, which primarily explains area deprivation . . . it also implies national action to remedy poverty – by incomes policy, full employment, less specialisation of work roles, higher social security benefits, new forms of allowances, a more redistributive tax structure, and a broader industrial ownership. [*New Statesman*, 6 August 1976]

Less spectacularly, evidence from other studies was also becoming available: from the preparatory work done for the CDP (see chapter 2), and from the Inner Area Studies in Lambeth, Birmingham and Liverpool. As Lyn Davies, himself closely associated with the Liverpool project, put it on a subsequent occasion,

the two strands – the debate on poverty and the questioning of urban renewal – came together in the summer of 1976. The catalysts, probably, were the intensifying unemployment notably becoming more of an intra than an inter regional problem; and the re-emergence of racial questions epitomised by the rise of the National Front and events in London's Southall and Notting Hill areas. Within the government, too, results were beginning to emerge from the long work of the Inner Area Studies and the Community Development Project, the day-by-day accretion of experience from fieldwork in the inner cities and the postulating of hypotheses about inequalities in society and the inadequacies of government action. [*Architects Journal*, 5 July 1978, p. 17]

The same two strands were also linked in an open letter addressed by Peter Walker to the Prime Minister. Walker, the initiator of the Inner Area Studies, had taken time off after the defeat of Edward Heath's government, with whose managerial approach he had been closely associated, to devote himself to the study of the problem of urban poverty and in particular its racial dimension. His conclusions were unequivocally pessimistic, and were clearly influenced by his experience in setting up the Inner Area Studies. As he observed,

successive governments, including your own, have operated in Britain general improvement areas, the priority
neighbourhood schemes, the housing action areas, the
educational priority areas, the urban aid programme, the
job creation programme, the youth employment scheme
and the community industry scheme. And yet I must tell
you that the help is not reaching this group of people who
needs it most. During the operation of all of these
schemes the unemployment has increased, the housing
conditions have got worse, the crime rate has soared to
new heights and we are making no substantial breakthrough as far as education is concerned. [*New Statesman*, 18 June 1976]

In his reply to Walker, the Prime Minister made it clear that
the government had been considering a new initiative. The
first public indication of the form that this would take
emerged with the news that a special working party of junior
ministers had been appointed to examine the problem (*The
Times*, 6 August 1976). In fact, as the account in the previous
chapter indicates, the appointment of this working party was
the culmination of a process of review that had begun the
previous August. The novelty lay in the Prime Minister's
decision, announced in the following month, that the chair of
the working party should be taken by Peter Shore, as Secretary of State for the Environment.

DRAWING UP A NEW POLICY

The Prime Minister's announcement of September 1976
closed a phase in the long rivalry between the Home Office
and the Department of the Environment which had begun
when the same James Callaghan had seized possession of the
original Urban Programme for the Home Office eight years
earlier. It also began the long-overdue process of
concentrating power and control over resources in one place,
the absence of which had helped to restrict the effectiveness of
previous initiatives. The initial direction of official thinking

emerged into the open with unusual rapidity: less than a week later, at the end of a tour of inner-urban areas outside London, Peter Shore laid down the broad lines of future policy in a major speech at Manchester. In it, he singled out quite unequivocally economic problems as the major issue with which any new initiative would have to be concerned. All the areas he had seen, the Secretary of State said, shared common problems. In the course of a long review of the causes of their decline, Shore attacked the 'general consensus', which he portrayed as having outlived its value, in part because the forecasts of a sharp increase in population had not materialized, in part because 'the planned efforts to decentralize and decongest the inner-city had been accompanied by a voluntary movement of people much greater than was anticipated by the planners'. Other changes had also been important in their effects on the inner-city economy; for example, 'road haulage has taken over from rail almost completely so far as secondary and tertiary industries are concerned, and with the building of inner-urban motorways peripheral locations have appeared to offer substantial advantages on transport grounds alone'. Planning and housing policies had also had an impact ('albeit unintended') on firms:

> comprehensive redevelopment schemes, uncertainty created by planning blight and well intentioned but perhaps over-rigorous efforts to remove 'non-conforming' industrial users from an area zoned for residential use have all led to the particularly small and medium ones. [DOE, 1976]

Yet despite this critique of past performance, Shore also warned against assuming that initiatives by government – either central or local – could be immediately effective:

> we have only limited power directly to create the industries, large or small, privately or publicly owned, on which the wealth of these areas will be based. All industries and firms are bound to take their location decisions according to which are likely to produce the best return.

Our effort must primarily be directed not so much to making those decisions but to influencing them, either in favour of or against the inner areas. [DOE, 1976]

New initiatives, he added, have up to now been only partly effective because 'they have to some extent dealt only with the symptoms and not the causes of the decline of the inner city. The causes lie primarily in their relative economic decline, in a major migration of people, often the most skilled, and in a major reduction in the number of jobs which are left.' A new approach should involve looking very closely 'at the operation of our planning mechanisms'. It would also be necessary to consider 'whether the incentives to industrial location could not be better tuned to assist the inner areas without disturbing regional policy'. New towns policy had also been represented as creaming off investment. 'I certainly acknowledge', Shore observed, 'that the objective circumstances in which the new and expanded towns are operating have changed, and it is these changes and not any criticisms of the past value of new towns which I do not question, which must cause us to reappraise their future role'. Hence, 'we do have to ask how far positive dispersal policies should continue when we can so clearly see that those who leave now will not be replaced'. All this should be seen against the general background of the significance of major cities, which 'serve and sustain the whole region around them in cultural, social and economic terms. If cities fail, so to a large extent does our society.' Remedies, when they emerged from the review that he proposed to undertake, would be as comprehensive as possible (DOE, 1976).

Shore's speech aroused great interest, tempered by some criticism, notably among the local authorities and in the Town and Country Planning Association, the traditional advocates of dispersal policy and defender of the new towns' interests, who had exhibited bitter hostility to the conclusions of the GLC review at the beginning of the same year.

Challenged by Peter Jay on television's 'Weekend World' programme in November, the Secretary of State responded sharply to suggestions that shortage of funds and vested interest within government departments would make it inordinately difficult to launch a significant initiative, and that he would do better to concentrate on an initiative 'within the trend', as Joe Rogaly of the *Financial Times* put it. Shore saw his objective as finding ways of 'tilting the balance back at least to a position of neutrality as between staying in the city environment and moving outside'. Answering Jay's objection that, with the reluctance to invest and very slow growth, it would be increasingly difficult to generate any substantial economic revival in the inner cities, Shore replied that, 'in a period of very low growth which we have at the present time, and a period of high national unemployment, there is a particular difficulty but one obviously is not going to base the strategy on the assumption that the present difficulties are going to continue for any serious period of time.' His approach would be based on checking the 'unexpected and accelerated exodus in the past few years. The main reason for this has been, in my view, the planning policies of local authorities and the underlying belief that everyone seemed to have until very recently that it was wholly proper and virtuous to encourage as many people as you possibly could to leave the inner cities'. He hoped to finish the full review that he had embarked upon within six months (transcript of 'Weekend World' interview, November 1976).

The Prime Minister's intention had been that the ministerial committee over which Shore was presiding should not be tied to conventional departmental lines but should work collectively to arrive at an overall view of the inner-city problem, a view not unduly uninhibited by departmental considerations. This was a potentially novel approach to a problem, the solution to which had been inhibited by departmental rivalry and vested interests. However, it had quickly become apparent that, despite the Prime Minister's wishes, the committee's main day-to-day work was being conducted on very conventional lines. The normal kind of departmental papers were presented to the Committee, explaining existing programmes and policies, and they closely resembled the Burns Committee papers. There were few indications of junior ministerial enthusiasms being allowed to exert any real influence.

Indeed, the Home Office junior minister on the Committee even felt obliged to request the Home Secretary's approval before presenting a paper on the CCP.

However, despite the similarity of the Shore Committee papers to those that had earlier come to the Burns Committee, there were clear signs that a more urgent approach was being adopted. Ministers accepted, for example, that very little would be achieved without a new commitment on the part of central and local government to the regeneration of the inner cities. Such a commitment would be judged by the willingness to implement new priorities, to make new funds available and to change policies. Like the earlier Burns Committee, the Shore Committee recognized the prime importance of main policies and programmes, all of which needed to be given an inner-city dimension. On finance the Committee was convinced that substantial extra resources needed to be made available to Partnership authorities: it was necessary to give the government's proposals credibility. The Committee also saw the need for continuing collective ministerial oversight of any new policy to secure an inner-city emphasis for various government programmes and policies and to resolve any disagreements on policy or priorities that might arise between departments. Some machinery might maintain a watching brief on the development of inner-urban policy and programmes on the city.

The main controversy surrounding the draft report of the Committee related to the question of finance and the redistribution that would be involved. Doubts were raised at the top of the Home Office about the realism of switching resources from shire countries to inner cities, given expenditure restrictions. That it should be the Home Office raising doubts illustrates the continued reluctance of that Department to back a concern about urban deprivation with real money. However, the DES was also concerned about finance. Its Secretary of State, Shirley Williams, had general reservations about the approach to the inner cities being advocated. Her Department had already offered substantial savings from school meals to help housing, and she made it clear that there was no question of finding more money. She referred to the potentially devastating effects on authorities like Cambridgeshire and Cumbria, and argued that the recommendations of the Layfield Report should be considered first before taking action on the inner-urban areas. Mrs Williams felt it would be both unjust and inept to finance the inner city from offsetting savings elsewhere in local government, particularly education, and indicated her opposition to the concept of helping inner-city areas largely at the expense of the education budget. When these concerns were eventually discussed at the Cabinet ministerial group on inner-city areas in March 1977, they did not prevent the endorsement of the general outlines of the Shore Report. However, the majority of the group was not in favour of drawing a close distinction between the Urban Programme and the new inner-city grant, and the Secretary of State for Environment was asked to consider a modified version of his report, encompassing a single programme of urban regeneration.

Meanwhile, the exact form of the policy was emerging by stages, not all of them determined by Peter Shore himself. In January 1977, the preliminary results of the three Inner Area Studies were circulated under cover of departmental circular to local authorities. In February 1977 Shore told the Gulbenkian Conference on the Inner City that 'in the field of planning and architecture more than perhaps in others we have suffered grievously from fashion, from conventional wisdoms which have become a substitute for serious and critical thought', and that we should approach the issue 'in a careful and considered way'. 'We must be concerned', he told his audience, which was drawn substantially from voluntary as well as statutory organizations, 'because the consequence of turning our back on the inner areas would, in my judgement, be likely to be mounting social bitterness, an increasing sense of alienation, worsening crime and vandalism, and, in some areas, racial tension as well.' The strategy that he laid down was along the lines of the Manchester blueprint:

> The first objective in my list would be to improve the local economies of the inner-city areas. In present-day conditions, when there is not very much brand new

commercial and industrial development, our top priority must be to preserve the jobs that at present exist – a vital task when one considers the high proportion of the loss of jobs arising from firms not moving out of the inner city but simply dying there.

Here, the role of small firms could be crucial. Other important initiatives would include 'industrial improvement areas, enabling old premises to be converted and new ones to be built in replacement of obsolete factories'. The second key objective would be to improve the social and physical environment. 'Because of the limitation of resources,' he warned, 'we shall have to be highly selective in deciding which areas deserve special attention. And once the choice is made close co-operation will be needed to ensure, on the one hand, that authorities have the necessary flexibility so that they can go for the right mix of measures, and on the other hand, that central government helps them to achieve this by reshaping the activities of its own departments and agencies to match.' Despite the importance of community initiatives and involvement, this emphasis on government was essential. This was because, 'if we are to make real headway in improving the conditions of our inner-city areas, we must use the main programmes of central and local government. We need to get an inner-city dimension into those programmes at central and local level alike.' To fuel this process 'some additional and carefully directed resources for the inner-city areas are needed' (DOE, 1977g).

The response of the conference was not excessively enthusiastic. Many of its membership inclined towards the view that the intervention of the government was at best a necessary evil, and at worst one of the causes of the problem.

A variant on this theme was provided by Professor Peter Hall, in an article published to coincide with the conference. He pointed out:

the inner cities have traditionally provided first homes – and first jobs – for immigrants. The East End of London successively attracted the Huguenots, the Irish, the Jews and now the people of Bangladesh. Each generated a distinct urban sub-economy. Most gave us a rich new entrepreneurial strain. Some of these new capitalists stayed small. Others prospered, grew large and left the ghetto. [Hall, 1977]

The conclusion was clear enough: 'why shouldn't the government see this and build on it?' The moral Hall drew was that the government should, in effect, reverse the basis of its immigration policy and try to attract more newcomers with the right skills and attitudes. As he himself forecast, his proposals were a little too rich for the Secretary of State's blood. Ironically, it was Hall's Enterprise Zone proposal, adapting the concept of a stimulus for entrepreneurial initiative to limited geographical areas, that caught on, but with a Conservative government.

Peter Shore's message did find a receptive audience in the local authorities. Their anxieties, as reflected by the Association of Municipal Authorities (AMA) (circular letter, 14 February 1977), were more down to earth. Were new resources on offer as a result of this new initiative? If so, how could they ensure that they were not excluded from the handout? (The Gadarene rush after Harold Wilson's urban programme speech of May 1968 was still fresh in many minds.) In consequence, the period leading up to the unveiling of the initiative in Parliament was punctuated by attempts to force the government to show its hand. Lengthy memoranda were prepared and submitted both by the AMA and by the Association of District Councils. Deputations from authorities outside London sped to Whitehall. Members of Parliament were put up at Westminister to reinforce the case: when the member of Liverpool, Garston (Mr Loyden) asked the Secretary of State to pay a visit to his constituency, Mr Shore's positive response was interpreted by other anxious members as a possible tilt in favour of Merseyside. The member for Henley interjected, 'is the Right Honourable Gentleman aware that while he is considering his review of these problems the situation on Merseyside is rapidly getting a great deal worse as a result of many policies of his government?' 'I do not agree,' Mr Shore told Mr Heseltine (*Hansard*, 16 March 1977, cols. 365–7).

When the announcement did come, it had been heavily discounted in advance and the usual dismissive phrases – 'peanuts', 'chickenfeed', 'tinsel' – had all been used freely by commentators, some of whom had to choke back their criticisms rather abruptly on seeing what was actually in the statement. Some of the impact was also dissipated by the fact that the resources element had been anticipated by the Chancellor of the Exchequer, who announced in his Budget statement of 29 March 1977 that he was setting aside £100 million for a package of construction works in selected inner-city areas. But the announcement that the Secretary of State had to make aroused very considerable interest – so much so that the debate on the statement fills an unusual 20 columns of *Hansard*, ending with the Speaker's rather lame explanation that he had allowed lengthy discussion 'because of the direct constituency interests', meaning in practice the desires of members, in good congressional style, to make good their claims for access to the pork barrel. Generally, the theme of concentration of resources on economic regeneration and partnership between local and central government commanded widespread support; but it was the location of the action that really interested members. Nor did the parallel announcement on new towns, indicating both a change of policy and a drastic cut-back of resources, attract the kind of criticism that might have been anticipated. Clearly, the form of the proposal presented some difficulty for the Opposition. Peter Walker's robust support could have been anticipated. Michael Heseltine's reaction was much more qualified and lukewarm (he had been critical of Shore's preference, as he presented it, for study over action). It was Reginald Eyre, as front bench spokesman, who unwittingly revealed the problem for his own side: 'would the Secretary of State', he asked, 'accept that the Opposition view with anxiety this proposal to continue using the needs element of the RSG to transfer money from country areas to the city?' (*Hansard*, 6 April 1977, cols. 1226–46). As Shore replied, fairly enough, it was hardly sufficient to will the end but not the means. Finally, the presentation of the new policy was rounded off by the publication in June 1977 of the Summary Report of the three Inner Area Studies and, earlier in the same month, by the release of the long-awaited White Paper.

THE WHITE PAPER

The originality of the White Paper approach, at least as reflected in successive ministerial announcements, rests essentially in its claim to be comprehensive. The White Paper itself opens and closes with this claim (DOE, 1977e, paras 3 and 98). The analysis of the problem facing the inner cities leans heavily on the Inner Area Studies, as might be expected, and has been described, not unfairly, as a good staff college exercise: not original, but a deft distillation of the newer conventional wisdom, allowing a primary role to the economic issues but stopping short of the rather rigid economic determinism of the CDP teams. When it comes to remedies, the White Paper is chock full of ritual genuflexions – to the importance of race relations, to the need for population balance, to the significance of public involvement, to the key role of private industry. But these are side issues: the crux is the machinery of government and how it can best be adapted to the new objective of securing the urban economic revival that the analysis requires.

The issue of harnessing a government machine divided by function to resolving a problem cutting across different programme areas was not exactly new. The CPRS had made a vigorous if not wholly successful assault on the same problem in their Joint Approach to Social Policy. Two powerful voices had drawn attention to the self-same issue in the course of the debate running up to the issues of the White Paper: in the report of the Gulbenkian Conference of February 1977, *Save Our Cities*, John Stewart was quoted as observing that, 'if we say that the central–local relationship is important in dealing with the inner-city, then we are saying that we have no machinery at the moment that is adequate for its handling. . . . it requires a change in the machinery of government

(Righter, 1977, p. 28). The Liverpool team, in its summary of its own report, had concluded that the best approach in the circumstances of Liverpool would probably be 'to make one of the existing bodies responsible for detailed planning and improvement of all those programmes directed specifically to the inner city, instilling commitment to an inner-area policy within the existing structure of government. Under this approach,' they argued,

> channelling resources to the areas of greater social need should be comparatively straightforward in theory. . . a committee for the inner area would control the allocation of central government resources and could organise the necessary delegation and reorientation of services for each neighbourhood.

These were bold claims: but the team had gone further. Economic development, team members added, might be an exception, and here

> a total approach will depend not on the institutional arrangements, or even on the level of resources allocated to the inner areas. The motivating force will lie in the strength of political commitment to the aims of inner-area policy and the degree to which administrative practices are capable of being adapted to the requirements of a total approach. [HMSO, 1977, pp 14–15]

The White Paper picks up this general emphasis but differs in detail by arguing for collaborative machinery including all agencies in every field, not merely those concerned with economic planning. Special machinery is justified as a means of achieving a more unified approach but retaining the individual contribution of all executive agencies. The inner-area programme is the instrument by which this is to be achieved. Besides the additional funding now made available for this purpose, central government proposed 'to develop a more co-ordinated approach to urban problems' (para. 33), and 'to ensure so far as practicable that their policies and programmes are given an inner-area dimension and priority in order to assist the regeneration of these areas' (para. 45). These assertions were to give central government representatives in those inner city partnerships established as a result of the White Paper considerable difficulty when the time came for the goods to be delivered.

In this way, the question of machinery was linked to the other major issue that had provoked such anxiety: the amount of resources likely to be made available. The White Paper resolved this problem by making confident assertions about the extent to which, in allocating the needs element of the rate support grant, the government could 'ensure that full account continues to be taken of the needs of authorities with severe urban problems' (para. 48). The credibility of such an approach clearly depended on the extent to which it would be possible to guarantee in advance the continued availability of resources over a significant period of time. Here, the difficulty was clear. To talk about ten-year time horizons, as the White Paper did, was simply not realistic in terms of recent British politics – or, indeed, of planning and budgetary procedures. Hence Shore's anxious appeal across the House in April 1977, seeking to invest the initiative with the insignia of bi-partisanship.

The other problematic issue was the use of that deeply unrealiable device, the rate support grant system, and the needs element within it (the Schleswig – Holstein question of modern British administration). For the meanwhile, the only secure and quantifiable source of funding was the special allocation: the £100 million interim construction package already made available by the Chancellor and the Urban Programme – increased from £30 million in 1976/77 to £125 million in 1979/80, and finally made the executive responsibility of the DOE.

The two key assertions of White Paper policy – the claim that the new initiative was not merely modestly incremental but was providing a new major source of funding, and the parallel concept of a comprehensive programme, integrating the activities of all relevant agencies – remained problematic, to be tested in the breach. The first test of these assertions came in the course of the negotiations with the eager aspirants for Partnership status, which began even before the legislation enabling the local authorities to take up their new role in economic regeneration had been put before the House.

A year after the White Paper had been published, Peter Shore delivered another speech, this time to the Royal Institution of Chartered Surveyors meeting at Harrogate. 'This is an appropriate time', he began, 'to take stock of what has been achieved so far and to look at directions for the future.' Repeating his previous claim with new emphasis, Shore asserted that 'this is the first comprehensive policy for the inner cities which this country has ever had'. None of the previous initiatives, he added,

> challenged the fundamental post-war trend of loss of population and jobs from the inner city, together with physical, social and economic decline. Our policy now is to halt that downward spiral; to strengthen the economic and social structures of the inner cities at the same time as we improve their physical environment; and to create confidence in the future of the inner cities as places to live, work and invest. The measures and the approach which we have adopted can only be understood in the light of this radically new objective. [DOE, 1978a]

Then he ran through the list of practical initiatives that had already been taken. The setting up of the seven Partnerships – Liverpool, Manchester and Salford, Birmingham, Newcastle–Gateshead, and three in London (Hackney–Islington, Lambeth and Docklands); the 15 other local authorities that had been offered special arrangements, later to be known as the Programme Authorities; the increase in urban programme funding, and 'perhaps the most important of our initiatives at national level so far'. the Inner Urban Areas Act, enabling designated local authorities to assist local industry – though not, he added at once, at the expense of regional policy. In a phrase he was to become very attached to, the Secretary of State saw himself by 1978 as having 'reversed the engines of decline'. How accurate was this claim proving to be in the field?

THE LAMBETH CASE

The selection of Lambeth as one of the Partnership areas stemmed not from the negotiations that took place in the aftermath of Peter Shore's announcement of April 1977, but from a decision taken five years earlier. When Peter Walker initiated his Inner Area Studies in the summer of 1972, a London study area was required: some interest had been displayed at that stage in and by Camden; the Kilburn area seemed worth exploring; but in the end of the decision went in favour of Lambeth.

Although Lambeth might at first sight seem to be a logical location for a 'deprivation study' (to use the terminology of the early 1970s), it was not at the time – nor is it now – the most deprived of the inner London boroughs. The borough is in fact a slice through inner south London, with the thin northern end of the wedge resting on the river and the broad end on the 'White Highlands' of Streatham. At the northern end, around Waterloo, large office blocks (the Shell building, County Hall) are interspersed with the remnants of nineteenth-century terraced housing. Comprehensive redevelopment has thinned out the population and left an uneven pattern of development, especially where gentrification has preserved some of the larger stuccoed terraces and squares. The centre of the borough – Brixton, around the town hall and market – forms the hub of south London's communications; around it settled the longest established West Indian community in London, now quite widely dispersed through the central area and largely housed in local authority blocks. But in central Lambeth, too, the large blocks of public housing and working-class terraced housing are interspersed with the survivors of some of the larger houses built for the Victorian middle class (the oases, in the terminology of the inner-area study). To the south of the borough the pattern changes again, with a predominance of more modern interwar and postwar developments, detached and semi-detached houses at lower density, substantially in owner-occupation and some blocks of flats, both public and private sector, among them. One of the four parliamentary constituencies invariably returns a Conservative member (Streatham); another (Norwood) has oscillated between the parties, being currently (1981) represented at the GLC by a Conservative councillor and at Westminster by a Labour MP. The two northern constituencies customarily remain firmly in Labour hands.

The borough, then newly returned to Labour control after an unexpected interval of Conservative rule (1968–71), had accepted the Inner Area Study, no doubt on the assumption that at the worst it might help form the basis of a bid for increased resources. The prospectus issued by the then Secretary of State for the Environment, Peter Walker, had stressed the need for a comprehensive approach and laid particular emphasis on the potential for action experiments, focusing on the physical environment as the primary centre of attention and incorporating any evaluation of the feasibility of special management schemes. The London consultants, Shankland Cox, invited the social scientist Peter Willmott, then at the Institute of Community Studies, to join them in preparing their preliminary assessment. The assessment, which was presented to a steering group of members of the London Borough of Lambeth and GLC and representatives of the DOE, accepted the basic framework laid down in the brief with the significant addition of a focus on the needs of the local population as established through an ambitious programme of surveys.

Thus, although the area selected for investigation was relatively small (the Stockwell area, with an estimated population of 60,000), the balance was already shifting in the direction of a people-rather than area-based focus. The study itself covered a wide range of issues affecting not only the borough, but inner London as a whole. Once commissioned, the investigation took a full three years (1973–76) and produced, in addition to the final report, a series of interim reports on different facets of the investigation. The sequence of publications served to sustain outside interest in an operation that had in a political sense gone cold after the departure of Peter Walker from the DOE, and the subsequent decision to set up the Urban Deprivation Unit at the Home Office as a focus for future activity.

The initial stress on action research faded rather rapidly, although some useful experiments were undertaken on the feasibility of the scheme for paying child-minders (the Groveway experiment). In general, the problems of funding experiments from an exiguous budget and the locus of responsibility for them after the completion of the study quickly quenched any enthusiasm that the study team and the steering committee had originally felt. The centrepiece of the study was therefore provided by the social survey, which gave the basic material for the final report as well as a platform for advocacy of a number of different initiatives – notably the teams controversial proposal for a programme of balanced dispersal. This survey was supplemented by a study of employment in the borough.

One of the most striking findings of the survey was the basic dissatisfaction of the resident population in the Stockwell study area with their neighbourhood. Forty-eight per cent of the residents in Stockwell said that they would 'prefer to move to another district'. Though some of those who said they wanted to move said that they would prefer to remain in inner London, the majority sought the semi-detached houses and green spaces of suburbia, which they contrasted with 'the overcrowding, the unloved blocks of council flats, the dirt and litter, the resented newcomers, the crime and vandalism of the inner city'. But there were exceptions to that general rule of discontent, which ran considerably higher than that expressed in broadly comparable surveys elsewhere. These exceptions were almost equally intriguing: recent immigrants to the area, both those from the New Commonwealth and the middle-class newcomers, were substantially more likely to express approval of the area. The reasons given for dissatisfaction also offered some pointers for new initiatives, notably the conflicts between adults and children and the need for more play facilities, and the concern about vandalism and crime. The issue of jobs did not loom as large as it would have done some five years later – the survey was conducted in 1973 – but the survey findings brought out clearly the association between lack of skills and lack of employment opportunities and the effects of disadvantage produced by racial discrimination.

More controversially, further analysis of the study's findings identified two distinct forms of poverty – income poverty and housing poverty – and suggested that the two were largely independent phenomena, at least in the special circumstances of Stockwell. The problems of low pay were exacerbated, the report suggested, by 'mis-match' between the skills of the local inhabitants and the jobs available in the inner London employment market.

The remedies seen by the study team included an attempt to correct the shortage of skills; dispersal of the population to open up opportunities not available to the unskilled; an end to disruptive major redevelopment schemes; the removal of restrictive legislation cramping London's scope for new economic initiatives (the Industrial Development Certificate and Office Development Permit system); and a substantial intervention by local government in the employment process (DOE, 1977b).

These findings became available in outline at the beginning of the period when the inner-city policy was being unveiled, and appeared to have some influence on the evolution of policy within the DOE. However, the most notable influence exerted by the study was in determining the choice of Lambeth as a Partnership area. From the beginning of the period of informal discussion that took place in the spring and early summer of 1977 about the selection of areas, it had been evident that in the DOE's eyes the fact that an Inner Area Study had taken place in an area was likely to be a vital argument in favour of an authority. The government placed particular emphasis on the desirability of monitoring the effectiveness of the new policy: clearly, the possession of adequate base-line information would assist in that task. Camden, now anxious to reverse the decision of 1972, found this particularly galling; however, the selection of Lambeth aroused less controversy than the pairing of Hackney and Islington for a second Partnership in North London.

Once the principle of participation had been accepted by Lambeth and the other local authorities concerned (GLC and ILEA), initial negotiations at ministerial level led rapidly to the setting up of a task force under the chairmanship of Lambeth's Chief Executive. This included a senior member of the

DOE's Inner-City Directorate, representatives of the other statutory agencies likely to become involved (besides the GLC and the ILEA, the Area Health Authority) and senior officers from the borough – the Director of Development and the newly appointed Corporate Planning and Programming Officer. The team had an outline blueprint before it from the DOE, but considerable discretion to modify the pattern to suit the particular local circumstances. The crucial decisions were the selection of the precise area to be covered by the Partnership arrangements, which in the light of the considerable variation in condition throughout the borough was assumed not to cover the whole area, and the setting up of the administrative machinery – the structure of committees and the creation of a full-time team to support them. The first issue was readily disposed of: the area of operation of Partnership was to be that part of the borough lying north of the South Circular Road, with the significant modification, insisted upon by the local authorities, that for purposes of employment and industrial promotion the whole borough should qualify. The basic committee structure was accepted as given in the DOE's proposals: first, a Partnership Committee chaired by a DOE junior minister (Guy Barnett, the Labour member for Greenwich), with representatives at junior minister level of other government departments with an executive interest (the Department of Transport, the Home Office, the DHSS, the DES, the Department of Industry, and the Department of Employment), and member-level representatives from the participating local authorities (Lambeth, GLC, ILEA) and the Area Health Authority, shadowed by an Officers' Steering Group (OSG) with equivalent membership, supported by a small Inner City Unit, with a full-time head of senior but not chief officer status, and the staff seconded from the main participating agencies.

The newly formed machinery was immediately put to its first test: the selection of schemes for funding under the Chancellor's special construction package initiative announced as part of the Budget earlier that year. The experience of putting together a programme, much of it ironically resurrected from among schemes deferred in the public expenditure cuts of the previous year, and the testing of the quality and feasibility of the schemes put forward, taxed the ingenuity and diplomacy of the Steering Group. But it was generally felt that the first test had been passed, and that collaboration was a feasible proposition.

By the time of the first meeting of the Ministerial Committee (28 Novermber 1977) the other initial hurdles had also been cleared: a senior officer from Southwark had been appointed head of the Inner City Unit, and located in the office of the borough's Chief Executive, who had been nominated as chairman of the Officers' Steering Group. Arrangements were in hand to second staff from the DOE, GLC and ILEA to provide the nucleus of a supporting team.

The next major decision, which fell initially to the OSG, was to recommend priorities for the Partnership's first full inner-area programme. It was intended that this should form the basic planning document of the Partnership, and provide by means of a rolling three-year programme the basis on which the grant allocated to the Partnership would be awarded. Two key decisions were needed: the programme of geographical areas to which priority should be attached; and the way in which funding should be allocated between them. At this stage, the report of the Inner Area Study should have come into its own; but in practice the OSG proceeded largely on instinct. Area priorities were discarded without argument: the choice of action on employment and housing was virtually automatic. But to balance these, two need-group-based programme areas were identified: 12- to 22-year-olds (with the problems of young blacks particularly in mind) and the under-fives. Sub-groups were established to cover each of these four areas and set to work to prepare submissions for the first programme, due to be considered by the Partnership Committee in the spring of 1978.

These initial decisions exerted a lasting influence on the operation of the Partnership – the conscious intention in the case of the second to identify issues that cut across departmental and agency boundaries through the identification of need groups was an important innovation. It followed (or appeared to follow) from that decision that the allocation of funds in the budget should be by topic priority rather than by agency. While this decision was arguably correct in terms of basic priorities, it posed serious problems for the infant Inner City Unit when it came to identifying responsible authorities and monitoring the implementation of projects. It also placed increasing strain on the impartiality of the local authority representatives on the Officers' Steering Group and Partnership Committee, torn between their attempt to ensure that their Partnership priorities were reflected in the draft programme and the pressure of their home departments and committees for a larger share of the resources.

Most of these problems, however, lay ahead. Progress in the early meetings was sufficiently rapid to enable the Unit to produce a draft inner-area programme for the meeting of the Partnership Committee in April 1978, and thereafter put it out to public consultation.

The issue that then arose was another that subsequently preoccupied the Partnership for long periods: how far should the public be involved in the actual decision-taking – what precisely should public consultation mean?

Lambeth Borough Council had been engaged for some time in an elaborate series of initiatives designed to secure public participation based on a series of neighbourhood councils. Despite these initiatives, it quickly became clear that the contribution of representative voluntary bodies could not be assembled with dispatch on a reasonably credible basis. In order to do so, and to secure the rapid response that was necessary, an umbrella group was formed, the Lambeth Inner City Consultative Group (LICCG). Meanwhile, the traditional device of a public meeting was adopted. In the event, this encounter with the public was not a success. The inner-city programme was attacked from all sides as heavy, indigestible, and deliberately confusing: both the intentions and the execution of schemes on the programme were sharply criticized, despite the inclusion of a substantial number of schemes that directly or indirectly assisted the voluntary sector. The parliamentary Under Secretary of State, present as chairman of the Partnership Committee, was given a thoroughly uncomfortable time. Undertakings had to be given that the procedure adopted for the future would be an entirely different one, providing adequate time for assessment and response.

The Lambeth borough members, too, were dissatisfied with what had been achieved. They felt that no clear priorities emerged from the jumble of schemes in the first programme. At best, the proposals were past rejects, still clogged with dust from the shelves on which they had rested. At worst, they were just more of the same – not at all what the new initiatives had promised. The 1978 borough council elections had led to the dislodging of the existing Labour leadership, which had been closely associated with the Inner Area Study and had developed a collaborative style that left ample scope for officer and official initiatives. The new leader, Ted Knight, and his committee chairmen wanted the whole exercise to be brought more firmly under political control and to be given the distinctive stamp of their own approach – the regeneration of the area through a substantial investment of funds in public sector initiatives. Their approach conflicted sharply with that of the GLC, Conservative controlled since 1977, and their representative on the Partnership Committee, its Deputy Leader, and by no means sat comfortably with the Labour government's own thinking. The political tensions that were set up as a result became increasingly sharp in the course of the discussions that took place in the autumn of 1978, and in particular during the run-up to the production of the second inner-area programme, covering the years 1980–83.

In response to criticism of the 1979–82 programme and the way in which it had been produced, officers had prepared a discussion document reviewing the difficulties that had arisen. The rushed preparation of the earlier submissions 'has always been justified by the need for visible and early action to establish the credibility of the Partnership', they contended.

Its achievement has none the less been at a cost in terms of the time allowed both for public and political consultation and for establishing the long-term direction and objectives of Partnership. With the completion of the first three-year programme, the Officers' Steering Group are anxious that the Committee should give some early guidance on the future direction of the Partnership to ensure that work in the coming year provides a firm and considered base for long-term achievement.

In the view of the Group, objectives could be set that 'could be useful as a means of clarifying the way forward', but there was a danger that the exercise could be counter-productive if made 'too onerous or grandiose'. On the other hand, it was agreed that each sub-group or exercise should have a clear remit or time-scale for each phase of its work. There was general agreement that in the next phase the Partnership should aim: (1) to initiate and monitor action arising from the considerations so far given to the four priority areas (housing, employment, under-fives and 12 to 22-year-olds); (2) to identify gaps or issues for further consideration in the light of public consultation and the experience of the first stage of the Partnership; (3) to develop further the closer cooperation and coordination between the agencies so far achieved. On consultation, the officers commented:

> there is still considerable dissatisfaction amongst the local groups about the level of their involvement, and they will be seeking in particular some participation in the formulation of strategy during the coming year. The establishment of the Lambeth Inner City Consultative Group, with its various sub-groups (e.g., housing, under-fives, physical decay), will prove useful in this respect.

And, they added, 'in addition to this the Borough Council will continue to press for the Partnership Committee to be open to the public' (Lambeth Partnership Paper, La ICPC (78), 20, unpublished). These proposals were then agreed by the Partnership Committee, and subgroup chairmen were set to work on the process of preparing a new programme for scru-tiny by members. The target they were given was to bring the second programme forward by the late spring of 1979 , thereby allowing a longer interval for consultation and amendment in accordance with the pledges given the previous year.

This second phase of activity uncovered a series of practical problems that had been largely skated over during the rush to prepare the first programme. The main motive force now lay in the subgroups: by this stage, they were being expected to generate new ideas and work them up into firm proposals for implementation; comment on the initiatives of constituent agencies; evaluate proposals from voluntary bodies seeking funding; and monitor the progress of projects already started in the first-year programme. In some cases the scope for action was substantial, either because the field was well mapped out (under -fives) or because it had not yet been trampled over and the scope for collaboration was considerable (employment). In other cases the existence of entrenched interests presented difficulties (the 'adolescents at risk', formerly 12 to 22's, contained representatives of two notoriously touchy bodies, the ILEA and the Metropolitan Police, both of them with well worn and conflicting interpretations on the increasingly difficult relationship between the adolescents in question and the local police), or conflict so acute as to preclude any possibility of progress (housing, with intractable contradiction between the policies of the GLC under Conservative control and those of the borough).

Although draft proposals were duly produced, and the process of reconciling competing claims completed without excessive friction, the political kaleidoscope was given another and decisive shake by the fall of the Labour government in May 1979. Meeting on a strictly provisional basis, pending a review of policy, the Partnership Committee under its new chairman, Tom King, Minister of Local Government, authorized the release of the draft 1980–83 programme in July 1979 for public consideration.

The substantial involvement of the voluntary sector in the preparation of the programme had secured a considerably higher proportion of funds for voluntary bodies; the likely outcome of consultation would have been more favourable still to them had it not been for the government's decision, announced in November 1979, to make a drastic cut in the allocation to the Partnership, from the original figure of £9.25

million to £6.66 million. The response to this not entirely unexpected announcement took two forms: first, a joint deputation to the Minister from all the local authorities involved asking for the restoration of at least part of the cut; and second, a public meeting with the leader of Lambeth Borough Council in the chair to protest against the likely impact of the cuts on the voluntary bodies whose share of the programme had risen to around 20 per cent. This large and impressive meeting was distinguished by the testimony given to the value of the Partnership and its support for voluntary organizations from a wide variety of different bodies of diverse sizes and compositions – stricking evidence, if nothing else, of the way in which opinion had swung round since the first consultative meeting, and a tribute to the range of contacts and individual relationships established by the energies of the Inner City Unit and by the LICCG, now equipped with a permanent full-time officer of its own. But neither tactic proved sufficient to deflect the determination of the Minister to trim back the programme, and a substantially revised budget had to be produced on a short time scale.

This stage of activity brought the issue of the vested interest of individual agencies again to the forefront: the attempt at the earlier stages to promote an inter-agency approach suffered a sharp setback. This was perhaps not surprising; nor was it to be wondered at that the voluntary agencies, un-represented at any level higher than the Officers' Steering Group, where they sat as observers only, were at a particular disadvantage when the cuts were being made. In addition, the prolonged and detailed scrutiny of individual cases by the DOE, sometimes as high as ministerial level, finally undermined the fiction that the Partnership was an exercise conducted on an equal basis as between equal partners, to which DOE officials at least had paid elaborate lip service at earlier stages. Moreover, it focused attention on two key weaknesses of the procedures to date: the failure to extend the area of concern to the crucial main programme activities of the major agencies operating in the area including those of central government, and the tendency of a rolling programme to 'silt up' with revenue projects. The 1979 crisis tilted the balance decisively against new staff-intensive initiatives and hence against the voluntary sector in which such schemes predominated.

On the first issue, strenuous attempts were made by local government representatives to raise issues of the effect of central government policy intervention on the locality. Two particular areas of policy aroused particular concern. The first was health, where the DHSS's attempt to put into effect the Resource Allocation Working Party's recommendations on the redistribution of resources within the health service led to cuts in inner London AHA budgets that were directly contrary to the proclaimed objective of harmonizing central government policies in favour of the inner city. The extent to which the DHSS was determined to impose reductions on 'over-resourced' areas (i.e., those containing or in proximity to a major teaching hospital) were somewhat startlingly underlined when the Southwark, Lambeth and Lewisham Area Health Authority was put into commission by the Secretary of State for the Social Services for refusing to reduce its budget. The AHA was accordingly no longer represented at Partnership meetings for a period of six months, only to reappear, like a demon king catapulting back through a trap door, when it emerged that the Secretary of State's action had been *ultra vires*.

A second area of similar concern was employment. Here, the initial success of the local government respresentatives in securing the extension of the area of eligibility to the whole of the borough proved to have been a pyrrhic victory. Attempts to secure some modifications of the rigidities of regional policy were resisted by the representatives of the central government departments concerned, the Department of Industry and the Department of Employment, whose often-repeated contention that national policy considerations overrode those of the inner-city policy proved impervious to the repetition of the White Paper formulae.

A more sympathetic approach was adopted by the Manpower Services Commission (MSC), whose London Regional Director played a substantial role at all the earlier stages of development of the London Partnerships. (This may have had something to do with the fact that London regions faced a variant of the same problem in attempting to establish the credibility of their own programmes with MSC colleagues in other regions.) Yet even the MSC was sometimes parsimonious in its concessions to the special case put forward by Lambeth, arguing, as the ILEA also tended to do, that its London-wide responsibilities ultimately overrode any allegiance to particular Partnerships. Nevertheless, employment policy remained an area in which the mutual suspicions of the local authorities were at a comparatively low level, and sufficient support was available from the other agencies to encourage the belief that programmes might be put forward. The subgroup on employment had in its early stages been very much strengthened by the arrival of the recently acquired Employment Promotion Officer for the borough, who acted in effect as their executive arm; and in the first year of its activity the employment subgroup had succeeded, as the 1980 Review Report put it, 'in creating a full employment programme funded through the IAP to fill a local need. Its wide membership, including community groups, provides the main forum on employment and industry in Lambeth. Its proposals for main programme work are dealt with directly by the relevant Council Committees. Support for its continuance is widespread' (Lambeth Partnership Officers' Steering Group, review of year 1980). By concentrating on manpower policies rather than on physical schemes, the group was able to show earlier results than some of their opposite numbers in the other Partnerships. But by 1980 the hopeful start was beginning to fade in the face of the crisis of the inner London economy, and the associated sharp rises in the rate of unemployment and job loss throughout the area. Invited to present a progress report to a special review for the Partnership Committee in 1980, the subgroup's Chairman was able to point to a number of achievements. 'The Partnership's employment programme in Lambeth', the group's report concluded,

> can claim the following successes to date: (1) to have related its programmes to the assessment of priority needs; (2) to have had a major impact on the provision of training facilities for young people and encouraged an industrial development programme which fully takes up

the opportunities of land resource in the borough; (3) to have fully committed its planned programme of Partnership expenditure, and to have taken up a proportion of slippage in other areas of the programme; (4) to have significantly used Partnership funding to attract main programme expenditure of over £2 million, mainly through the MSC, but also Department of Industry and the GLC and LBL, an important principle in the use of the Partnership resources. [Report to the Employment Subgroup, June 1980, La ICPC (80) 45]

But the rate of unemployment continued inexorably upwards, and increasingly disturbing evidence accumulated of the relatively disadvantaged position of young blacks. Energetic lobbying by the voluntary organizations, directly or through the Consortium of Ethnic Minorities, produced a series of voluntary sector schemes; but useful though many of these proved to be, they were insufficient in scale to do more than mop away at the edge of the growing problem.

The revised draft of the 1980–83 programme summed up the argument about the past performance and future direction of the Partnership.

The achievements of the Partnership in 1978–79 can be seen as its progress in bringing agencies together in joint projects and the consideration of issues; the involvement of the voluntary sector, particularly the black community; and in encouraging employment and economic regeneration initiatives. Early experience also raised several fundamental issues which remain to be answered. For example, how extensive is the commitment to involving the community in policy-making and resource allocation by all the Partnership agencies? Also, how far should inter-agency main programme policy conflicts between both local and central agencies be pursued through the Partnership machinery? The ability of the Partnership to initiate radical approaches is also a matter for constant consideration. In addition, other subjects have not been considered fully by the Partnership. No framework has yet emerged for work on many aspects of social deprivation. There has been little progress on reviewing main programmes and achieving a redirection of resources towards the inner area where this is not already the case, or in setting up projects jointly managed by the community and a statutory agency [Lambeth Inner Area Programme, 1980–83]

The initial review of the Partnership programmes conducted by the incoming Conservative government had pointed to other weaknesses: the tendency for meetings to become over-large, over-protracted and ends in themselves; the diffusion of emphasis by willingness to fund a little bit of everything; and what appeared to some ministers to be a tendency to stifle real innovation in the voluntary sector by discouraging self-help through excessive emphasis on providing paid staff.

EVALUATING THE EXPERIMENT

The first three years in Lambeth: some general conclusions

Considered as an experimental period, the first three years of the Lambeth Partnership had produced a number of useful new initiatives, besides providing the inevitable learning experience for all involved. The emphasis on the voluntary sector – whose effective spokesmen were, however, never allowed access to meetings (or even the full papers) of Partnership Committee – clearly had considerable value in producing schemes that would not otherwise have been funded. A significant proportion of these were put forward by black organizations – the roll-call of grants provided for the Scarman Inquiry is impressive, at least at first sight.

At the end of the day, however, the vested interests of the local authority departments in all the agencies concerned ensured that the voluntary sector could hold only a minority interest, and that the cuts would fall disproportionately on them rather than on statutory schemes. Yet the quality of these schemes and their relevance to the objectives of the

Partnership was never tested with sufficient rigour, despite all the efforts of the Inner City Unit.

For the technical and managerial emphasis of the earlier stages of Partnership, inherited from the consultants' study and sanctioned by the tone of the White Paper, seemed increasingly out of place in a higher political situation. At the earlier stages, a sense of common objectives and the prospect of additional resources produced, as had been intended, a willingness to compromise in the interest of making progress. The diplomatic skills of the GLC's Deputy Leader, Richard Brew, had made a particularly important contribution at this stage. But by 1980 the growing economic crisis and the sharpening of political conflicts destroyed much of the confidence that the participants had initially felt in each other's intentions. At times of outright confrontation between the London Borough of Lambeth and the Secretary of State for the Environment, the fact that they were joined together in Partnership no longer seemed a very relevant consideration.

As for the Secretary of State himself, or his successive representatives on the Partnership Committee – Tom King until 1981 and subsequently Lord Bellwin – one clear-cut revelation of the workings of the Lambeth Partnership was how far he had to function, in Whitehall terms, as *primus inter pares* with his ministerial colleagues rather than the 'supremo' of which the newspaper headlines of 1977 had spoken. The failure of central government departments to deliver more than the most grudging or token support was a major departure from the comprehensive approach proposed in the White Paper, and one that local government did not fail to bring home at every conceivable opportunity. Tactically, the effect of constant pressure of this kind was undoubtedly counterproductive: departmental ministers took to appearing for the minimum period possible, at two meetings a year. After the change of power at Westminster, even this minimum commitment disappeared: one Labour MP, commenting sarcastically in the House about poor attendance at the Lambeth Partnership, asked the Minister of Local Government if there had been a race meeting that day. When ministers did appear they were flanked by permanent officials and determined to give nothing away. Those who attended stuck firmly to the principle of the primacy of departmental priorities, or attempted to assert that the issues with which their department was concerned were nothing to do with local government (social security policy was a case in point). The promised co-ordination of effort (the key feature of the White Paper) clearly had very little visible effect when it came to particular cases.

There remains the question of resources. One school of thought has argued that the funds made available were by design too small to make a real impact, but large enough to be an attractive source of rivalry. Perhaps this statement contains a kernel of truth; but to present this as a deliberate feature of policy is excessively cynical, given the economic pressures that existed when the policy was devised and under which it has been carried out. It also overlooks the fact that, for a voluntary organization, a relatively small sum can spell the difference between survival and collapse. The rapid growth of activity and the wide range of initiatives funded provide impressive evidence of the flexibility and responsiveness of the voluntary sector, at least for the period when significant attempts were being made to promote its involvement. The statutory agencies, too, have some positive achievements to which they can point – for example, in the field of employment generation.

Yet by mid–1980 the verdict on the Lambeth Partnership had to be a sceptical 'not proven': the Conservative government's reservations had been freely expressed; several of the statutory agencies were beginning to wonder whether the game was worth the candle; and the voluntary sector had been disillusioned by the differential impact of the cuts. But by that time Peter Short, too, had made his own assessment; and as originator of the policy his views should be heard before an attempt is made to pull the threads together.

Peter Shore's assessment

Six months after leaving office, Peter Shore took the opportunity presented by an invitation to deliver the Thomas Cubitt lecture to provide a comprehensive defence of his record in the area of urban policy (Shore, 1980). This in itself was an unusual procedure: politicians out of office with new responsibilities are not always anxious to return to the scene of their previous activities. The analysis that Shore provided was not in itself especially striking: but it provides a convenient set of bench-marks against which to measure the success and the failures of inner-city policy during his period of office.

The lecture itself consists of a rather over-hasty summary of the analysis that produced the impetus for the new policy development; an account of the measures actually introduced, the rationale underpinning them and some distinctly modest proposals for their modification in the light of early experience. The features of the presentation that are of particular interest are three. First, there is a greater degree of emphasis on environmental issues: 'as the tide of prosperity and economic activity has ebbed from the inner-city,' Shore comments, 'the social and physical features of decay have emerged'. And he adds, 'apart from the high incidence of crime and vandalism, I can think of nothing more characteristic of inner-city decay than the pervasive graffiti that cover walls, pavings, pillar-boxes, houses and flats in our inner urban areas'. Unemployment, though clearly seen as a major consequence of the decline that Shore describes, does not present itself as the first priority for immediate intervention.

The second notable feature of the case presented is the vigorous defence of the machinery set up as a result of the inner-city initiatives, and in particular the formation of the Partnership apparatus. In describing his critics, he said: 'there are some in local government, but only a small minority, who believe that government under the Partnership arrangements is impinging unnecessarily on local government functions on autonomy. There are some who say that the arrangements are cumbersome and bureaucratic. There are those outside the central local government Partnership, in the voluntary sector, who believe that they should be directly and strongly represented on Partnership committees'. He goes on, 'I am not persuaded by any of these criticisms,' and proceeds to attack the new Conservative government's proposals for development corporations on the grounds that such an initiative necessarily requires the consent of the local authority in whose area it is to operate if it is to be successful: 'if the proposal for a UDC is negotiated with the local authorities and is accepted by them, well and good. If not, if it is simply imposed, it will be the cause of dissension, resistance and delay; it simply will not work.'

So the link between central and local government, arrived at by consent rather than coercion, is still an essential part of Shore's concept. Yet there is also a recognition that the relationship has not functioned entirely satisfactorily. In particular, the criticism of the contribution by central government main programmes to the objective of Partnership, so frequently raised by local authority partners, is to some extent conceded. 'I am not satisfied', Shore observes, 'that expenditure on health services has responded to the deliberate "bending" of programmes in support of inner-city areas.' This leads him to propose 'not the holus-bolus scrapping of RAWP, but a sensitive modification of its allocations within regions, particularly inner London, in favour of the inner cities.' Rather less radically, Shore appears to endorse by omission the view that other agencies of central government had done their share. Finally, on resources, Shore claims that 'the cities (and London in particular) have been greatly helped.' Yet, he adds, 'while the present rate support grant system does undoubtedly help the cities, it is not sufficiently accurate to concentrate upon those most disadvantaged in our great conurbations.'

With the modifications implied by these comments, Shore concludes his lecture with a call for continuity in policy 'for a period of at least a decade ahead. For confidence is the key, and only a long-term government commitment can supply it.'

Subsequent developments and their impact

To some degree, his successor as Secretary of State, Michael Heseltine, has shown himself willing to supply that longer-term commitment. Heseltine's initial review of the programme led him to the conclusion that it was 'unwieldy and over-bureaucratic' in its organization, but that with some minor streamlining the Partnership initiatives could continue in broadly the same form. His statement of objectives differs hardly at all from that of his predecessor:

> The inner cities are vitally important to the health of the country. We cannot have the thriving society we are trying to achieve if we have the inner cities decaying at the heart of it. We cannot afford the waste of resources of people and of land represented by areas of dereliction and desolation around our city centres. We want to make it possible for growth and prosperity to return to the inner city again. [*Architects Journal*, July 1980]

The distinctive special flavour is conferred by the setting up of Urban Development Corporations for the Liverpool and London docklands provided for in the controversial Local Government Planning and Land Act of 1980 and by the creation of Enterprise Zones. This initiative stands somewhat apart from the mainstream of inner-city policy, having been introduced – like the 1977 inner-city construction packages – not by the Secretary of State, but by the Chancellor of the Exchequer. The paternity of the Enterprise Zones is in some dispute: some trace the concept to Peter Hall, others to a speech made by Sir Geoffrey Howe in Opposition. In essence the Zones, initially seven in number and small in size (500 acres), represent another attempt at demonstration, severely limited in scope and hence (arguably) in application: the objective is to show that the removal of planning restrictions and generous subsidies to entrepreneurial enterprise can create the conditions for economic regeneration, Hong Kong style.

Enterprise Zones apart, the inner-city programme remained largely unchanged under the Conservative government with the crucial qualification that the reductions in public expenditure introduced affected the programme, though to a lesser degree than might have been anticipated. Although the cuts inflicted were not large – £7 million in the 1979–80 allocation, followed by a drop of £11.3 million in the 1980–81 allocation over 1979–80 (*Hansard*, 3 June 80) – the Partnership and programme authorities at a vital stage in their planning as they attempted to develop new initiatives. Much more significant was the Secretary of State's decision to reverse the general tilt in rate support grant in favour of inner-city authorities (and in particular London). This had a drastic effect on the main programme budgets of the London Partnership authorities, in particular.

The effects of the reversal took time to become fully apparent; but by 1982 (strictly outside the scope of this essay) they were clearly visible. Stewart Lansley, in a detailed examination of the process published in *New Society* (22 April 1982), concluded that in 1981–82, after allowing for the special penalties – known as 'holdback' – applied to those authorities exceeding the government's spending targets, Partnership authorities lost no less than £166.2 million in grant compared with 1980–81 – a cut of 17 per cent, which is nearly double the national average cut of 9.7 per cent.

Moreover, the average reduction hides wide variations among particular authorities. Five inner London boroughs lost more than a quarter: Islington (51 per cent), Tower Hamlets (35.7 per cent), Lambeth (27.6 per cent), Greenwich (27.2 per cent) and Southwark (26.4 per cent).

In the particular case of housing, Lansley found that over the four years from 1979–80 to 1982–83, Housing Investment Programme (HIP) allocations to partnership areas were cut by 47 per cent, compared with a national cut of 50 per cent. Some authorities were hit particularly heavily, notably Southwark (down 59 per cent in real terms), Greenwich (down 58 per cent), Gateshead (down 56) and Newcastle (down 54).

One of the symptoms of the stress generated by these progressive reductions was the conflict that arose between the Secretary of State and some of the authorities identified as 'high spenders', among them Lambeth and Hackney, which tended further to complicate relationships in Partnership between local and central government representatives.

Thus, despite Heseltine's formal re-endorsement of the policy in February, by the spring of 1981 the future of the inner-city policy had been compromised not so much by shifts in the basic policy objectives as by events on the broader stage of national policy. Indeed, the notion of a distinctive inner-city policy, with particular objectives imposed where possible across other programme priorities and reflected in the budgetary allocations both to programmes and geographical areas, had begun to fade from sight altogether. The programme was becoming a residual operation, a mere departmental initiative funded from a restrictive budget, much like the traditional Urban Programme on its original 1968 objectives had been. Indeed, one possible strategy that the Conservative government had already considered (but rejected) was to make that traditional Urban Programme redundant, and a consultative document was issued, offering among other alternatives that option.

Then, on the night of 10–11 April 1981, a series of major disturbances broke out in central Brixton in the heart of the Lambeth Partnership area. As a result of these events the scope and content of the debate on the inner-city changed into a different and higher gear.

DRAWING UP THE BALANCE SHEET

The period from September 1976 to April 1981 can be seen as one distinct and separate episode in the evolution of inner-city policy. Even if it has not satisfied Peter Shore's plea for a decade of stability in policy in which to establish the credibility of his own initiatives, it does provide a long enough time span to attempt to answer three key questions. First, was the 1976 analysis an accurate diagnosis of the problem that had emerged? Second, were the cures established in the 1977 White Paper appropriate to those problems? And, third, how far have they been administered, and, where they have, with what results? The remainder of this essay is devoted to these three themes.

First, the diagnosis. It would be generally agreed that in identifying the economic decline of major conurbations as the key issue with which urban policy has to grapple, Shore and his advisers had seized the right end of the stick. However, a number of qualifications were offered, from a variety of different quarters. The first was that the decline was not equally distributed between and within regions, and affected conurbations in different ways according to their basic industrial structure. Some conurbations exhibited substantial 'eddies' in the receding tide – the case of London is often quoted in this context. The growth of service industry and office employment alongside the decline of manufacturing industry has caused the effects to fall differentially upon the capital's population both by area and by occupational group (all this has tended to be masked by the habitual use of regional or even conurbation statistics in the debate). Second, the focus on major conurbations has tended to exclude discussion of decline in some of the medium-sized and smaller towns, particularly heavily affected by decline in traditional industry (the omission of Wales from the Partnership initiatives is a case in point). The inner-city focus in the analysis also tends to divert attention from the problems of peripheral areas – notably, the satellite public housing estates (for example, in Glasgow).

These are modifications rather than basic disagreements in the analysis: the critique from the left is of a rather more fundamental character. This holds that the 1977 White Paper analysis, while welcome in recognizing the basic economic causes as an explanation of the growth of poverty rather than individual pathology or a focus on distinctive problems of small areas, tends to place far too much emphasis on economic developments in a regional or sub-regional frame of reference without considering the causes and consequences of national economic decline. As a result of Britain's poor economic performance and the general impact of the crisis in developed Western economies, many of the key events affecting the country's economy take place outside the range of the British government's influence. This was demonstrated, it is argued, most dramatically by the substantial cuts in public expenditure made in 1976 at the behest of the International Monetary Fund, but also over a period of time by the decline in key sectors of British industry as a result of decisions taken by multinational corporations whose centres of operation lie outside the control of Whitehall. One example often cited is the motor car industry – the Chrysler company's activities in Coventry, extensively studied by the CDP, or Ford, whose decisions on the location of their British activities caused such anguish to the Callaghan government in its last days. Similarly, the innovations in high technology, to which planners have looked as a substitute for traditional manufacturing industry, are often dominated by international corporations whose decisions on future location of activity will be influenced by such factors as the availability of a docile labour force content to accept low wages, such as can be found in some Third World countries. Hence, attempts to redistribute resources on the basis of priorities defined at Westminster, either inter or intra-regionally, and using the machinery of national or local government, are, in this analysis, certain to prove inadequate, because the location of the problem has been mis-identified.

The converse of this critique is the one that eventually emerged, though only in muted form, in the Conservative government's initial statements (September 1979): that any attempt to institute economic regeneration directly through state intervention must be viewed with extreme scepticism (though this school of thought also asserts that the state, central and local, can exert a powerful influence on the health of local economies in a negative direction, and is often one of the root causes of the problem). The emphasis here is on a stringent review of the role and scope of state action, in relation to its cost and effectiveness.

With these important qualifications, the basic approach of the White Paper – frequently identified as 'corporatist' or 'managerialist' – has generally been conceded to be a realistic one. What of the attempt at remedies? The reliance on the existing machinery of government through a systematic attempt to impose a new form of coordination has been one key area of debate. A strictly pragmatic criticism of this form of approach has been that central government has never in the past been good at initiating and sustaining programmes that cut across departmental boundaries. The CPRS's response to this problem – the blue-print for a Joint Approach to Social Policy – ran into the sands; overlap and even conflict between departmental initiatives in neighbouring areas of policy remain commonplace. Hence, any new initiative that rests on the concept of coordinated introduction of new resources by different central government agencies starts with a major structural obstacle still in place.

By giving primacy to the role of central government – as both originating and implementing co-ordination – the approach adopted for the 1977 White Paper policy gives little play to the notion of local government initiative. Yet it is arguable that in the field of economic regeneration, the key area of innovation, many of the initiatives taken up in the period after the White Paper derived from experiments launched by individual local authorities – the industrial improvement area concept pioneered in Rochdale; the injection of funds into local industry in Tyne and Wear; the employment-planning policy document produced by Newcastle – all of which predate the White Paper and its analysis. Perhaps most striking of all, the GLC's initially derided attempt to introduce an economic planning role for local government into the arena of the Layfield Inquiry into the Greater London Development Plan (1969–71) had within five years become a new planning orthodoxy. The 'reversal of the engines of decline' through withdrawal by local authorities from town expansion schemes also predates Shore's own Manchester conversion – both Birmingham and London had already taken that decision. By locating the policy initiatives at the top level of Partnership, at least by implication, the 1977 policy risked limiting the scope for innovation.

So the emphasis of the Shore approach can be seen as essentially 'top down' in a situation where the top, in this instance the government departments, is not in the best position to make its interventions effective. The performance of central government in the three years since underlines the point. Shore himself concedes the failure of the health service to evolve a positive contribution to the inner-city policy; rather, the record shows that crucial resources have been removed from certain Partnership areas in pursuit of departmental policy goals of a different character. He is more sanguine about industrial policy: but Paul Lawless's helpful analysis shows that this optimism has little or no foundation. His account covers two aspects of industrial policy: regional policy as a whole; and the activities of the National Enterprise Board. On the first, Lawless concludes that

> the Department of Industry might in recent years have made marginal modifications in the spatial distribution of its resources to the benefit of the inner areas, but it has been a notably limited transformation and the impression remains that it is, perhaps rightly so, committed to national economic growth, and whatever spatial dimensions it adheres to are regional and certainly not inner city in scope. [Lawless, 1981, pp. 127–8]

On the latter, he observes that 'the overriding impression given by the NEB, both through its formal objectives and in an analysis of its investment patterns, is that it has had a minimal impact on the inner areas which, considering the institutional, financial and political constraints imposed upon it, is not at all surprising'. This comment reflects the situation before Sir Keith Joseph imposed a further drastic reduction in the scale and extent of regional policy.

This leaves only the manpower budget, administered through the MSC. Here there is some evidence of a continuing response to the lead given by the DOE: but this is hardly surprising, given the fact that the MSC is the only central government agency to have been operating on an expanding rather than a contracting budget over the three-year period (a hiccup on the arrival of the Conservative government having been rapidly eliminated once the extent of the rise in unemployment became evident).

The scope of the resources concerned makes the issue of main programme priorities crucial to any evaluation. Given, as has just been demonstrated, that most central government main programmes have been almost completely insensitive to the priorities set in the White Paper, how about local government main programmes? Here, two issues arose: first, the question of crude priorities for Partnerships where only part of a local authority area was identified for action: second, the issue of the transfer of funds within local authority budgets between programmes to match the broad Partnership priorities identified for the three-year rolling programmes.

In the London case, both the GLC and the ILEA, operating over much larger geographical areas, were reluctant to concede any degree of priority to the areas selected by the movement for special status. Indeed, in the GLC case there was some talk of a 'countervailing role' in favour of boroughs whose legitimate claims to inclusion had been overlooked – though there was more rhetoric than substance in these statements. Local authorities at all levels faced a real difficulty, however, in allocating priority in main programmes, in the shape of increasing restrictions on the resources available over the period, especially after the Conservative's had reversed Peter Shore's 'tilt' in favour of urban authorities, including the Partnership and programme authorities.[1] This development was bitterly resented. The London borough of Islington went so far as to issue a special document with the hopeful title of 'Islington's reasoned case for government support' (1980), but to little avail.

These restrictions on resources meant that the substantive effects of the inner-city policy were almost entirely confined, after the first year, to the additional expenditure made possible by the enhanced Urban Programme. The difficulties here were two-fold. First, there was the matter of scale. Even when distributed to a limited number of areas, the restricted levels of resources available implied very substantial limitations on the freedom to take new initiatives. This freedom was further curtailed by the not entirely unexpected tendency on the part of local authorities to use the funds either to re-float schemes that had been shelved during the course of the previous rounds of public expenditure cuts, or, increasingly, to reinforce those areas that had been subject to further reductions in the current rounds. And, finally, the area of major innovation in employment policy fell precisely where local government had the least experience and the most limited powers to achieve change – even with the reinforcement provided by the Inner Urban Areas Act of 1978. In local government financial theology, the Urban Programme (Traditional and enhanced) ranks as a specific grant, and hence qualifies for the disapproval of the local authority associations. Nevertheless, most of the beneficiaries would have been prepared in prin-

ciple to go along with a specific grant in this area provided that
the strings attached were not drawn too tight. This, however,
was exactly what began to happen as the central government
cuts were imposed.

Until that occurred, the arguments centred not on the
justification for the existence of a special Urban Programme,
but on the selection of the priorities for the allocation of funds.
Initially the major area of debate was over the identification of
areas for Partnership status. Shore is cavalier about this in his
Thomas Cubitt lecture: 'It is, of course, in such an approach
essential to make choices. Yet in spite of the breach of the
block grant principle, and in spite of the competing claims of
other inner-city areas, the seven principal areas of need, the
Partnership areas, virtually selected themselves, and were
hardly challenged.' In fact, there was a groundswell of considerable discontent at the choices made. First, it was argued
that London had done rather better than it should have done
(it did not go unremarked that not only the Secretary of State,
but also two of his junior ministers who were closely associated
with the Partnership programme, were London members);
this, despite the fact that the identification of precise areas
within a large conurbation for Partnership status posed major
problems of rationality and consistency, especially in terms of
economic programmes. As has already been implied in the
Lambeth case, it was suggested that the original identification
of the Inner Area Study areas was altogether too influential.
And the omission of South Yorkshire, the East Midlands and
South Wales from the top tier suggested to the Association of
District Councils in particular that the emphasis on large
urban areas had been altogether too all-enveloping. Some of
the edge was taken off this last criticism by the identification
of the 15 programme authorities, but it remained a continuing
grievance.

The content of the rolling three-year inner-area programmes as they emerged from the first round of Partnership
discussions was also a focus for criticism. The bare bones of
expenditure allocations suggest that the White Paper goal of
primacy for economic regeneration was far from being
achieved. This reflected in part the fact that in the initial

process of preparation a premium was placed on schemes already prepared for implementation (the 'off-the-shelf' projects already referred to). It also reflected the problems of translating broad policy goals into action in areas where local government had few powers and usually less experience. The basic statement of principles prepared by each Partnership as the first part of its inner-area programme was little help here: in order to achieve consensus, the objectives tended to be stated so broadly as to be capable of covering almost any form of action. The factual analysis provided with the objectives was in general quite useful, but suffered from a deficiency of data stemming from the government's decision to cancel the 1976 sample census (a decision deplored in the Cubitt Lecture by Shore, himself a member of the Cabinet that took it). Finally, the priority for economic regeneration would in any case have been hard to translate into action since not all the agencies concerned with implementing it were represented within the Partnerships or accessible to their influence. The government's Departments had by and large escaped the need to accept Partnership objectives, even in a ritual sense, as has already been demonstrated; the private sector was only peripherally involved, and the trades unions, not at all. Hence the typical Partnership could not hope to coerce the one, or entice the others.

What was required (it was agreed) was a firmer lead from the DOE to colleagues in other government departments, notably the Department of Industry; more incentives to the private sector over and above those in the Inner Urban Area Act (the Enterprise Zones represent a further step down this path, but on a miniscule geographical scale); further inducements to local authorities to engage in joint initiatives with the private sector; and the expansion of entrepreneurial effort involving voluntary organizations of the type experimented with by the Manpower Services Commision in the course of its special programmes initiatives. Some of these elements were present in the programmes devised by the employment sub-committees of a number of the Partnerships. As we have seen, the Lambeth case was one of those in which such initiatives did take place. Even if nothing else had been achieved as a

TABLE 5
URBAN PROGRAMME ALLOCATIONS BY PARTNERSHIP AUTHORITY, 1979–82

Schemes	Docklands	Hackney/Islington	Lambeth	Birmingham	Liverpool	Manchester/Salford	Newcastle/Gateshead*	Total
Economy								
£'000	15,288	4,164	1,813	8,555	12,205	8,151	1,079	51,256
%	27%	13.8%	10.4%	32.4%	27.9%	18.9%	13.9%	22.8%
Housing								
£'000	200	1,177	1,030	4,844	6,914	809	965	14,939
%	0.4%	3%	0.1%	18.3%	15.8%	1.9%	12.3%	6.6%
Physical Environment								
£'000	4,959	3,569	2,557	2,093	13,522	4,385	316	31,404
%	8.8%	11.7%	14.8%	8.0%	30.9%	10.1%	4.0%	14.0%
Social Environment								
£'000	9,825	9,359	2,642	3,585	5,972	14,295	1,535	47,215
%	17.4%	30%	15.2%	13.6%	13.7%	33.1%	19.7%	21.0%
Leisure Community & Rec. Opportunities								
£'000	9,713	4,032	3,093	2,498	3,584	4,391	2,195	29,507
%	17.1%	13.2%	17.9%	'9.5%	8.1%	10.1%	18.1%	13.0%
Transportation								
£'000	13,361	2,936	-	2,422	171	408	1,212	20,780
%	24.0%	9.0%	-	9.1%	0.4%	1.0%	15.6%	9.2%
Voluntary Group Allocation								
£'000	3,000	2,269	3,929	2,422	1,410	3,799	499	17,328
%	5.3%	7.4%	22.6%	9.1%	3.2%	8.9%	6.4%	7.6%
Other								
£'000	-	2,638	3,300	-	-	6,905	-	12,843
%		8.6%	19.0%			16.0%		5.8%
Total								
£'000	56,616	30,144	17,366	26,419	43,778	43,143	7,804	225,271
%	100%	100%	100%	100%	100%	100%	100%	100%

* For Newcastle/Gateshead, figures are for 1979/80.
Source: R. Nabarro (1980), 'Inner city partnerships', *Town Planning Review*, vol 51, no. 1, p. 29.

result of the White Paper, these initiatives could provide some justification for the new departure in policy.

But generally, the inner-city programmes contained too many main programme items pushed across for the Partnership funding, either covertly or overtly. Some chief officers saw the Partnership or programme authority funds as a private pot of gold that could be used for their own pet programmes, and were often bewildered when other agencies questioned the value of such expenditure. Too many of these conflicts were resolved by the institution of quota arrangements, to be filled up by the department or authority nominated, and subject only to the rubber-stamping process of approval at Officers' Steering Group and Partnership Committee. Attempts to re-impose the concept of priorities stretching across the contributions of the different agencies fell to the Inner City Units (in London) and the DOE Regional Secretariats outside London. They were rarely successful in achieving more than marginal alterations, and in at least one case – the Brixton Recreation Centre – attempts to hold the line proved vulnerable to back-door political appeals for exceptions to be made, when the Secretary of State for the Environment authorized expenditure for Urban Programme resources on a main programme item.

The abandonment of earlier attempts to impose priorities hastened the process that had posed difficulties from the outset – the clogging up of the programme with the recurrent revenue commitments. This posed particular difficulty with staff-intensive voluntary sector schemes (although some local authorities too were guilty of supplementing their payrolls at Partnership expense): it led speedily to a situation in which very few new initiatives could be funded except at the expense of existing ones. A belated push by the DOE in the direction of funding capital schemes was seen as an attempt to discriminate against the voluntary sector; and anxieties were not quelled by the decision of Conservative ministers to set aside time for detailed scrutiny of individual voluntary sector items. The problem for the voluntary sector was compounded by the fact that it was difficult to identify convincing schemes to put forward in areas of maximum priority, notably economic regeneration.

The restiveness of the voluntary sector spilled over into criticisms of the machinery of Partnership itself. By the end of the second year it was widely acknowledged that the elaborate machinery of Partnership Committee, Officers' Steering Group and supporting sub-committees was too cumbersome. Increasingly, it was also seen as excluding many of those who had a legitimate role to play. The voluntary sector had felt this almost from the outset: Peter Shore's line had, however, always been that the new machinery would need time to establish itself before representation could be wider. The voluntary sector found his successor, initially at least, no more sympathetic on this score. Perhaps even more crudely, there was some evidence – in Lambeth, at least – that the local authority members found themselves excluded from policy formation. Their attempts to assert the primacy of their own committee machinery over that of Partnerships led to a number of sharp clashes in the London Partnerships, both within the Partnership Committee and at the officer level. One major difficulty was the absence of a distinctive focus of identity and action for the Partnership reflecting a single considered view. The secretariats were in general too weak: the experiment in Hackney–Islington with a coordinator at chief officer level failed almost immediately. DOE officials seemed to be in two minds about whether to play the role of partner or holder of the purse strings. Their juniors, inserted into Partnerships on the basis that they would at least provide good experience for fast-stream administrators, learnt quickly that there were limits on how far central government's writ could be made to run. Without a strong central core, the tendency for Partnership to avoid policy issues that would promote dangerous tensions, and to concentrate on non-contentious questions or allocation of extra funds, became steadily more marked.

These tensions clearly contributed in part to the case for the Urban Development Corporations, which had indeed, as Peter Shore made clear, been considered at an earlier stage. His agnosticism on the issue led him to the conclusion, already quoted, that UDCs could be acceptable in cases where local authority consent was forthcoming – the Scottish experience in Glasgow with GEAR provided some substantiation for this line. More broadly, though, a case for the consensus remained, despite its general failure to achieve incisive new policy initiatives. By forcing local authorities to work together, Partnership produced a new basis for collaboration, especially on occasions where they coalesced against central government agencies who had failed to contribute to the inner-city programme. This collaboration sometimes extended outside the range of Partnership initiatives, strictly construed. In Lambeth this was particularly true with the sub-groups, which were in general more effective than organizations higher up the pyramid in identifying common ground as a basis for action. Even in Lambeth, however, the identification of common ground in housing policy between a Conservative GLC and a Labour borough proved to be beyond the wit of Partnership. Central government representatives at this level, unable to modify their Departments' policy lines when under pressure, often found themselves in difficulty in public discussion, but were sometimes prepared to be more malleable in private. In addition, the problems of implementation, often understated from the comfortable distance of a Whitehall office, sometimes came into clearer focus for central government representatives, with interesting consequences. This was true even in the case of the Treasury, traditionally reluctant to soil its hands with anything as vulgar as a translation of macro-economic policy into action. At one London Partnership meeting the suggestion that Treasury officials might care to attend Partnership meetings in order to evaluate the problems involved in translating their guidelines into action was treated with derision by other central government officials – as well try to send for the Ministry of Defence to discuss the local implications of central government policy on national defence issues, one of them observed facetiously. Within 18 months, however, Treasury officials were seated around the same table discussing early implementation of the Chancellor's 'Enterprise Zone initiatives. What effect this will have had on the Pliatsky doctrine – that you cannot estimate from Great George Street what the effects of 'pulling a lever in Whitehall' is likely to have 'out there' – remains to be seen.

From the perspective of the voluntary sector, closer involvement also had some advantages. Nearer acquaintance with the machinery of Partnership provoked some justified criticism of the sluggishness of the machine, but this was balanced with some additional understanding of the problems associated with the implementation of new projects and the accountability for public funds. In the Lambeth case the existence of an effective umbrella body, the LICCG, with an articulate and determined full-time worker (paid for from Partnership funds) to coordinate the voluntary factor's response, led to the creation of a shadow structure of sub-committees parallelling the official machinery. The involvement of the representatives on these sub-committees with their opposite numbers helped to provide a coherent set of voluntary sector views at crucial stages in the planning cycle, and to ensure that worthwhile projects were brought forward and argued for at the right stage in the process. Here again, however, the impact of the cuts was extremely damaging: the voluntary sector feeling, not entirely without reason, that local authority officials were concerned to protect their own programmes and the staff associated with them, and consequently were prepared to allow the voluntary sector to take an unfair proportion of the cuts. These and other anxieties were reflected in the major meeting on the cuts in the Lambeth Partnership in the winter of 1979–80.

If the allocation of funds in Partnership was generally agreed to be less than totally satisfactory, there has been less agreement on the alternatives. Possibilities advanced at various stages have been the channelling of whole or part of the funds available direct to the voluntary sector, by-passing the intermediate (or 'buffering') role of local government; or the selection of one area of priority for the investment of the totality of the funds – smaller geographical areas (the central Brixton area in the Lambeth case?) a need group (under-fives or ethnic minorities have been suggested at various times), or a programme area (the inner-city economy – a community investment fund). A similar approach was cautiously mooted in the DOE's consultation document on the traditional Urban Programme, but no great interest was expressed, and the government decided to retain the programme in substantially its present form. The notion of the enhanced Urban Programme as a specific race relations fund also raised a number of fundamental difficulties. As Shore points out,

> race and immigration do not in themselves reflect or create inner-city decay. Indeed, in many areas – in Slough, in Southwark, in Leicester – their presence is more an indicator of growth and expansion than of decline and decay; while in Glasgow, Newcastle and Liverpool marked inner-city decay has taken place without the presence of a significant number of black immigrants. [Shore, 1980, p.8][2]

Any form of programme that isolates a group in the inner city for preferential treatment is also likely to be extremely controversial. This is clearly demonstrated by the last Labour government's attempt to up-date section 11 of the 1966 Local Government Act to produce a new ethnic grants system. A likelier avenue for action in the race relations field is provided by the attempts being made to secure the implementation of section 71 of the 1976 Race Relations Act, which lays a duty on local authorities to secure the elimination of racial discrimination in their areas. Securing the reflection of that obligation in the initiatives of the constituent agencies of the Lambeth Partnership was one of the proposals put forward to Partnership by the borough council's Race Relations Unit.

There remains the issue of spatial concentration: can a policy concentrating on a limited number of geographical areas ever function satisfactorily? Or, alternatively, is further concentration the only way of securing a real impact? Townsend's critique has already been quoted; it remains the strongest statement of the case for concentrating the effort at the national level. Yet the antithesis that has been made between local and national initiatives is in many ways a misleading one. Some programmes are necessarily spatial in their emphasis and need to be initiated at the level of the locality – housing and environmental programmes are an obvious case in point. Even economic programmes have strong spatial implications – perfect mobility of labour is not an objective that governments should necessarily be seeking to achieve. Some element of bringing jobs to localities (the underlying rationale of post-war regional policy) needs to be retained in any new policy. Hence Shore's emphasis on deprived areas and securing the 'richest mix' of policies for them is on the right lines: the problem is how to balance the elements in the mix. With the onset of rapid economic decline, the contextual industrial and employment problems are clearly going to assume greater significance, and the problem of giving any remedial measures a distinctive element of priority for areas in particular need is likely to become even more difficult. Yet the need for remedial programmes for especially hard-hit areas – not necessarily only those in the centre of cities – is becoming even more urgent. This problem of balance between spatial and contextual issues remains one of the major unresolved issues in inner-city policy.

Finally, Shore's insistence on continuity is well taken. If any single lesson emerges clearly from the account of successive inner-city policies, it is of the failure to learn from and apply experience gained at each stage. The process of policy development, so far from being an incremental one, has zig-zagged from side to side as the initiative has passed from one political party in government to the other and from one government department to another. If the broad lines of Shore's own approach and the gloss upon it suggested in this essay were broadly acceptable, his plea for a sufficient period of time to test the policies he introduced in 1977 would have some chance of success. Alas, all experience so far suggests otherwise: that the inner-city policy will eventually join the CDP and CCP and the whole alphabet soup of past initiatives in the scrapyard of redundant experiments.

6

Themes and Issues

One of the objectives of this book, as we indicated in the Introduction, has been to spell out some of the lessons (for theory and policy) that can be learned from more than a decade of experimentation and innovation in urban policy. This final chapter summarizes these lessons and draws out various themes that have emerged from the individual chapters.

One of the most important questions, at the theoretical level is how far these accounts of the different programmes bear out existing theories of social policy-making. It is clear that they do not substantiate the arguments found in some of the literature that they were aspects of a conspiracy to silence the poor, and part of some carefully orchestrated policy to avert discontent among potentially disruptive groups. The location of the early programmes in the Home Office, for example, did not reflect any particularly sinister motives. They were seen not as part of its law and order functions but, in the first instance, simply as an extension of the activities of the Children's Department. The civil servants who had been most active in drafting proposals for CDP were senior officials in the Children's Department, and it seemed a reasonable notion to site the new programme there. At the same time, a new venture with all the potential that the CDP appeared to have, in its early stages, would outweigh some of the more negative 'policing' functions of the Home Office. As far as the Urban Programme was concerned, because of its links with race and immigration policy, the Home Office again (as the Department responsible for these policy areas) seemed its natural home. Later, when the theme of coordination came to the fore, only the Home Office was expected to have sufficient 'clout' to be able to achieve any degree of inter-departmental cooperation.

As Banting observes, the extensive literature on policy-making identifies essentially four possible sets of determinants that may influence policy change: first the role of political parties and party doctrine; second, the preferences of 'the public at large'; third the impact of administrators and administrative structures; and finally, inter-group conflict. It is, of course, notoriously difficult to identify, with any degree of precision, the predominant influences upon policy at any particular point in time. Policy does not exist, in a pure form, independently of those who make it or influence it. It is a matter of interpretation as much as of statute, and it has both subjective and objective qualities. Consequently, what policy *is* , and whose particular ideas have shaped and fashioned it, are open to considerable dispute. Added to this is the further problem of official secrecy in Whitehall. The Official Secrets Act, together with less formal Whitehall conventions, mean that accounts by 'insiders' about the workings of the policy process may be considerably circumscribed while those of 'outsiders' can be dismissed as ill-informed. As a result, as Heclo and Wildavsky, observe:

> The political – administrative culture of British central government is a shadowy realm usually left to chance observations in politicians' memoirs or civil servants' valedictories. . . . probably less is known about the characteristic behaviour of civil servants and their political masters than about fertility cults of ancient tribes. [Heclo and Wildavsky, 1974, p.xix]

Despite these real limitations, it has been possible, in the earlier chapters, to draw some tentative conclusions about who makes policy and how.

The case studies of different programmes suggest that it was the influence of administrators and administrative structures that tended to predominate, especially in the early years. The evidence collected here seems to support the view that: 'The real battles over public policy were fought within and between, large departments well hidden from public view. Other political forces are crushed under the sheer weight of the administrative structure' (Banting, 1979, p.8). Civil servants, in many cases, did not adopt a neutral stance and were actively involved in orchestrating support for their particular proposals. This was especially obvious in the Community Development Project, with the central involvement of Derek Morrell and other civil servants in the Children's Department, but it was present to greater and lesser degrees in each of the programmes. Much of what emerged, in policy terms, was the result of inter-departmental rivalry, and did not augur well for a genuinely coordinated approach to the cities, as Malcolm Wicks observes in chapter 4, 'Furthermore, other factors – traditions and conventions, public spending patterns, planning systems, civil service career structure and training – militated either explicitly or implicitly against the joint comprehensive approach.' If civil service and other administrative influences were crucial in the evolution of the programmes, the implication would seem to be that the other potentially important groups in the policy-making process – political parties, the voting public and pressure groups – had correspondingly less impact. Again, the evidence seems to suggest that this was, in fact, the case.

There has been relatively little party political interest in urban policies and almost none in the earlier programmes. There were few questions in the House about the Community Development Project and Urban Programme, and they were not major items of political controversy even at key periods such as Harold Wilson's initial announcement of the Urban Programme or when the CDP fell into disarray. Urban policy generally has not figured largely in party manifestos, and until the mid-1970's, when a significant turning point does seem to have been reached, few politicians were identified with 'urban' or 'inner-city' issues. One of the exceptions – Alex Lyon, a junior minister in the Home Office who consistently tried to push these questions to the fore – argued on a number of

occasions that ministers were, at best, indifferent to the programmes for which they were responsible. With the shift of
responsibility for urban policies to the Department of the
Environment around 1976, a new burst of enthusiasm at the
political and ministerial level does seem to have taken place.
Peter Shore, in particular, became closely associated with
inner-city policy between 1976 and 1979 and especially with
the White Paper 'Policy for the Inner Cities', while Michael
Heseltine (as a result of the riots of 1981) has taken an interest
in such matters. Generally speaking, then, although few of the
initiatives came from politicians in the late 1960s and early
1970s, they have played a greater and more positive role from
the mid-1970s onwards. It is still a matter of speculation,
however, whether ideas for policy came from the politicians
themselves or whether they were essentially mouthpieces for
civil servants working behind the scenes. The evidence in this
book tends to support the conclusion of Heclo and Wildavsky,
in their study of the public expenditure process, that:

Rare in any system will be the policy which results from a
minister's bright idea never thought of before, carried on
his shoulders over the bodies of his officials, through the
dark valley of Treasury review and upward to final
Cabinet triumph. [Heclo and Wildavsky, 1974, p. 375].

However, in the final analysis, the relationship between ministers and their civil servants is constantly changing. It is a
question of personalities as well as of professional responsibilities and the exact nature of the relationship will vary from
individual to individual and Department to Department. In
the end:

the answer to the great question of ministerial versus civil
service power turns out to be so prosaic that no one is
really interested in hearing it. Sometimes ministers are
more powerful than officials in regard to certain areas of
decisions; sometimes the reverse is true; and sometimes
neither is in charge, however much they may pretend to
the contrary. [Heclo and Wildavsky, 1974, p. 376]

As far as the other possible influences on policy are concerned, pressure group interest (almost inevitably, given the many dimensions of urban deprivation) was relatively small. While different pressure groups took an interest in different aspects of the problem (low pay, housing, policing, the loss of jobs), few, if any, had a synoptic interest in urban areas or urban policy as a whole. The fact that the 'inner-city problem' had something in it for everybody meant that no single interest group saw it as its prime responsibility to act as watchdog over the urban policy process. At different stages in the process certain interest groups (such as the local authorities, the voluntary sector and private industry) had some impact on policy, but they were never the dominant sources of influence overall.

The voting public, throughout the 1970s, played little part in the debate (despite the general elections that took place). There were periodic outcries after specific incidents (such as the Enoch Powell speech and, later, the riots) and demands that 'something must be done', but there was no sustained commitment to reform. It seems likely that, for many voters, it was the 'single issue' that concerned them most, and few of those living outside the inner cities appeared to view the problem in the round.

The role of intellectuals and academics was not great. The Central Policy Review Staff was vocal in promoting the notion of co-ordination and a 'joint approach to social policy', but it was, of course, unable to ensure that these principles would be realized in practice. Some academics were involved at early stages in the programmes, reporting back on American experiences and so on. Later they made some contribution to independent evaluations of the programme but, overall, their influence was not great.

From all this it seems fairly clear that it was the civil servants who sustained the momentum of change in urban policy and who kept the concept of 'the inner city' alive. They were influential both when programmes succeeded and – as in the case of the CCP – when they failed.

All the programmes described in this book are examples of the particular brand of incrementalism that, according to

Heclo and Wildavsky, characterizes much of the public expenditure process in British government. Because such a large proportion of the total budget is committed in advance, there is room only for very limited manoeuvrability at the margins. As Sir William Armstrong observed, the very highest figure that most civil servants would accept as the degree of leeway was 2½ per cent of total public expenditure, and many thought that even this was an overestimate. Heclo and Wildavsky conclude that it is

> not merely that some expenditures are so committed as to permit only marginal change; it is that virtually all expenditure decision-making instinctively concentrates at these margins. Incrementalism in expenditure is understood and taken for granted by all British political administrators. They know it, live with it, and employ it in their daily work. [Heclo and Wildavsky, 1974, p. 25].

The programmes in this book can be seen as marginal in at least two senses. They were marginal to the primary policy concern of the Departments in which they were located (this was especially true of the Home Office programmes), but they were also marginal in expenditure terms and could not be allowed to threaten the integrity of existing and established programmes. At best, they were further examples of 'disjointed incrementalism' or – very occasionally – of what Wildavsky has called 'radical incrementalism'. They illustrate the strict constraints under which government, in the 1970s, felt itself to be operating, and the very limited horizons that policy-makers felt able to explore. They also illustrate the inability (or unwillingness) of central government to engage in long-term, problem-orientated planning at an inter-departmental level. Territorial jealousies and rivalry effectively put paid to genuine collaborative work, and the multi-faceted aspects of urban deprivation were never satisfactorily confronted.

COORDINATION AND MACHINERY

The various episodes covered in the course of the individual chapters chart a crab-wise progression on the part of central government towards the goal of more effective coordination. The obstacles in the path of achieving such coordination have repeatedly proved to be formidable: for example, John Edwards shows (p. 64) how the original intention of setting up a coordinated urban programme failed almost immediately as the programme fell apart into its constituent elements. Malcolm Wicks demonstrates how the attempt of the Home Office to improve on its past performance in launching the CCP experiment also foundered almost immediately (chapter 4). Even the latest initiative, the 'inner-city policy' – intended those currently responsible for it stress, not as an experiment but as a fully fledged programme – has run into the same sorts of difficulties (chapter 5). On occasions, the difficulties have reached a farcical pitch. The rivalry between the Home Office and the DOE for the central role and their corresponding eagerness to see off their opponents' new initiatives by withholding support at crucial stages is a constant feature of the first decade of urban policy (witness the episode of the appointment of the unfortunate Charles Morris as Minister for Urban Affairs in chapter 4). Resultant duplication of experimental initiatives in the early 1970s was a serious obstacle to progress, both through the wasting of scarce resources and because such experience as was gathered was not properly exploited.

Matters improved in the middle 1970s, in part as a result of the new managerial style that rapidly penetrated government, with its emphasis on the importance of machinery and relationships between its constituent parts, and on the effective marshalling of resources. Although the major lasting impact of this approach was at another level of government – in local authorities – the large-scale re-organizations in Whitehall that created the super departments (DOE, DHSS) and the *quangos*, many of them subsequently to perish at the hands of the political party that begat them, also had their impact on the area of inner-city policy – both in the concentration of power, which reduced the number of different interests that needed to be conciliated, and in focusing attention on common objectives and on outputs. (Movement in the direction of coordination was also accelerated by the impatience felt in several quarters, notably at the Treasury, about the wastefulness of overlap and rivalry in the previous phase.)

The first fruit of this new approach, the PAR described in chapter 4, led only to the abortive CCP initiative: but the broadening of emphasis in the attempt to sweep up all the relevant functions within one initiative led naturally to the fine flowering of the managerialist approach, the inner-city policy of 1977 (chapter 5). That this too should have failed to achieve the objective of coordination, as its begetter acknowledged, suggests at least the possibility that the blockage may be insurmountable. Yet there is nothing intrinsically implausible about the process of defining common policy objectives across departmental boundaries and securing the compliance of individual Departments to achieving common goals. Local government, at an admittedly smaller scale, can show considerable success in moving in this direction over the period of the 1970s, if at the cost of substituting a certain blandness in the product for the distinctive approach of the barons of the old pseudo-feudal local system. Perhaps more to the point, the Scots within a somewhat different structure of local and central government can also point to success in this area (GEAR?).

Why, then, has central government in England found it so much harder to move in the same direction? Three reasons suggest themselves.

1   Nobody has really believed sufficiently strongly in the importance of the objective. One of us has referred to coordination as 'an administrative opiate' (John Edwards, p. 64). True, it has been one of the standard pieties, honoured in the abstract but not seriously attempted in practice, except in a purely ritual sense. Documents emerging from joint exercises are said, with a wink and nudge, to be 'coordinated with a staple'. But once additional resources ceased to flow – effectively, in the second half of the 1970s – only minimum goodwill remained to be tapped for initiatives that could have been acceptable in circumstances of expansion. In Whitehall, the departmental culture requires loyalty to the principles of departmental policy not to some vaguely enunciated broad strategy (a point repeatedly illustrated in the course of the inner-city policy – chapter 5). This appears to hold good even

if the policy in question has been blessed at Cabinet level. To get on, the ambitious civil servant goes along with his departmental views – it is, after all, his Permanent Secretary who will judge his performance at the end of the day. Similarly, in the political field, ministers have to frame their objectives in departmental terms since their political future depends on their performance on departmental matters, both in the House and in Cabinet. Fighting their corner and defending their main spending programme leaves little inclination for fancy programmes for which others will enjoy the credit. Cabinet committees are all very well as places for discussion of policy priorities: but as a means of securing compliance with those objectives they barely begin to function effectively. The CPRS fills an advisory, not an executive, role; in this field its members have been spectators and analysts of failure, not promotors and sustainers of new initiatives. The Treasury, which does have a cross-cutting role, has used it primarily in a restrictive sense to try to secure as many reductions in the level of public expenditure in this field as possible. Coordination, in short, is contrary to the nature of the Whitehall beast, because what is everyone's business is no one's business.

2   The second explanation is that the levers that should have delivered coordination through connecting different parts of the machine failed because the machine was seizing up. Leo Pliatsky talked of the problem of securing compliance with policy goals set at the centre when local government fell outside the range of central government's control (quoted in chapter 5). Increasingly in the 1970s, central government moved towards a closer relationship with local authorities that would have among its benefits the securing of compliance with central government's priorities – explicitly, its economic policies. The days when the AMC could see off the Home Office and its admittedly feeble attempts to set priorities soon passed. Economic stringency turned local authorities into client statelets whose involvement could be purchased, at a price. But clienthood brought with it resentment at the role and a desire to kick over the traces as soon as a convenient opportunity arose. The partnership of which the 1977 White Paper made so much turned out to be like the motto of the old

Central African Federation – partnership, but between the rider and the horse. What has been true of the relationship between local and central government has been equally true if not more so of the voluntary organizations' relationships with local government. In the circumstances, coordination could not help but be a ramshackle affair, always likely to be overturned by the latest outbreak of ill feeling between local authorities and ministers (especially when they were under different political control, as was the case at several crucial stages during the evolution of the policy). Strong pressure from below from dissatisfied local groups, impatient with the compromises and delays involved in cooperation, further added to the complexities of the situation. In the Urban Development Corporations, central government's disillusionment with its experience took tangible form.

3 Finally, in some policy areas the means for coordination simply has not existed, in any practical sense. This is especially true in the area of economic regeneration. Apart from the influence exerted from agencies outside control of the British government altogether (IMF, multinational corporations), the possibility of a government of any political complexion securing a major change of direction in the investment policies of large British companies in favour of inner-city areas was never exactly high.

For this and other reasons, it is hardly to be wondered at that in the latest phase of inner-city policy the emphasis has swung right back to individual initiatives by a single minister with a personal and political commitment to change. The Merseyside Task Force (the term echoes, perhaps deliberatly, the American experiences of the Johnson administration) is a reversion to the highly visible style, using publicity and exhortation, directed in this case to the private rather than the public sector in order to achieve momentum. Once this has been done, the expectation is that other agencies will be swept up willy-nilly in the wake, without damaging compromises having to be made. This approach has the merit of permitting clear-cut policy objectives to be set, unfuzzed by compromises characteristic of coordination. Nevertheless, such initiatives have proved in the past to have limited staying power once their proponents have left office. It is the small-scale, uncontroversial, marginally useful initiatives that survive, half un-noticed – section 11, Urban Programme.

THE AREA APPROACH

Though an area dimension to public policy can be traced at least as far back as the postwar Barlow and Scott Reports, so far as the inner city is concerned, it first appeared in 1966 with Section 11 of the Local Government Act, to be followed in 1967–68 by the Educational Priority Areas (in reality, educational priority *schools*) and in 1968–69 by the Urban Programme. We have seen in chapter 3 how the idea of urban 'black spots' or 'needlepoints' of deprivation entered the thinking-out of the UP but how, for administrative convenience and the needs of defensibility, it was abandoned in favour of an approach that left the selection of recipient areas to local authorities. However, while no attempt was made to *designate* priority areas, it was expected that the additional funds would find their way into the 'small pockets' of deprivation.

The thinking that justified this form of resource distribution (and informed both the EPAs and CDP as well as the UP) was that urban deprivation was a residual problem of the welfare state, and that it consisted of geographical concentrations of poor and inadequate people locked in a cycle of deprivation or a culture of poverty. While it would not be true to say – as some have – that this diagnosis imputed fault to those in deprivation (the analysis was never that coherent or detailed), there was an implicit assumption that the problem was one of individuals and families, and that its cause (perhaps misfortune, perhaps inadequacy) lay with them or at least with their environment. To the extent that these 'victims' were concentrated in particular areas, then, the problem of urban deprivation was also thus contained, in both its causes and its manifestations, and the appropriate policy response was one that directed help at these areas. This was the essence of the UP approach. The CDP, being an experimental programme, was, as we have seen, organizationally different from the UP, but the same thinking underlay it and the problem (and solutions) were still thought to be spatially contained.

Though the CDP began with a 'pathology' diagnosis of urban deprivation, the analysis that was later to emerge from the action teams was a very different one. The problem was no longer rooted in individual pathologies, and though the manifestations may have shown spatial concentration, the causes would not be found in the areas within which the teams operated. Rather, they lay in local, national and even international economies. To try to solve them by injecting human and financial resources into localized areas was therefore futile. As we have seen (chapter 2), as the analyses became more radical so did the embarrassment suffered by the Home Office, with the ultimate result of the premature winding up of the experiment.

The new orthodoxy, which for convenience we shall call the 'structural diagnosis', had taken wider root, however, and it was perhaps inevitable that the reports of the three Inner Area Studies that so influenced the 1977 White Paper should reflect it. Once this diagnosis had gained currency and been legitimated by inclusion in the White Paper, a policy response of injecting small funds into small areas for a wide range of palliative projects was no longer credible. Whether or not this signalled the end of the area approach as such we shall examine below.

There was one other major influence on the demise of the belief that urban deprivation was a geographically residual problem that could be solved by directing extra resources to small areas. This was the accumulating evidence on the relative *lack* of geographical concentration shown by common indicators of deprivation (Holtermann, 1975a; Barnes, 1974). Even if the 'pathology' diagnosis had survived, tackling the problem by injecting additional resources into small areas was simply a very inefficient way of reaching the deprived. Many who were not deprived in these areas would benefit, and the great majority of the deprived, who, it was now clear, lived outside the inner cities, would not benefit at all.

The post-1977 policies – with the exception of the residual Traditional Urban Programme – were designed to fit the new structural diagnosis. If the causes of the inner-city problem lay not with deprived people but in the decaying economic infrastructure of inner areas and in the ramifications of national and international economic policies, then simple area-resource allocation could not be credibly maintained as a solution. This did not, however, result in the total demise of an area approach. The Partnership and Programme arrangements were established in those authorities deemed to suffer the worst deprivation, and the inner-area programmes – as we have seen – are mainly location-orientated. Similarly, the ill-fated notion of 'bending' main programmes was to have been a bending in favour of inner areas rather than of particular groups in the population who may or may not be geographically grouped. Of course, it may be argued that inner-city policies must inevitably be spatial policies, but while some certainly will be – notably, housing and environmental policies – there is no necessary reason why (for example) employment or education policies should be area-based, or why policies should not be directed at changing those housing allocation systems that help to create social areas of which inner cities represent one (diverse) form. There is a real difference between area-based policies and policies that recognize that urban social systems have spatial components and that resource distribution, whether planned or through the market, has spatial consequences.

Clearly, then, though policy responses changed after 1977, the area approach was maintained. The form that it took under the Partnership and Programme arrangements, however – the designated areas under the 1978 Inner Urban Areas Act, the Enterprise Zones and the Urban Development Corporations – was different from that under preceding programmes; and to understand this change we need to look at the ways in which positive discrimination operates in respect of areas. There are two different but related conceptions of positive discrimination. The first is whether discrimination is area- or non-area based; the second concerns the manner in which the discrimination is made. The first conception is clear enough; we may discriminate in favour of particular areas (regions, towns, wards) and hence in favour of all those living in the area (which is not to say that all will benefit equally from the positive discrimination); or we may discriminate in favour of groups in the population not defined on an area basis (ethnic minorities, the disabled etc.). The second conception is concerned with the manner in which discrimination is exercised, rather than its targets. Miller (1973) has identified three types of positive discrimination: preferences, allocational priorities and incentives. Until 1977, inner-city policy (mainly in the form of the Urban Programme) consisted of allocational priorities to small areas. As the effectiveness of this strategy was brought into question and new policies were developed after 1977, so the form that discrimination took changed, from allocational priorities for small areas to incentives to attract investment back into larger ones – the more broadly defined inner cities. The provision of such incentives may be seen as one of the key functions of current policies. While the method of positive discrimination changed, the area approach itself was not abandoned.

Thus, the move from allocational priorities to incentives predated the application of 'new right' economic theory to the inner cities from 1979, but such a move fitted perfectly with the requirements of Conservative government ideology, quite apart from the damage that a rigorous retrenchment in public expenditure would have done to a policy built around allocational priorities. While incentive payments to commerce and industry are a departure from pure market theory, they are more defensible than allocative priorities, both in terms of the 'new right' ideology and as a form of positive discrimination. Presentationally it is more defensible to exercise positive discrimination to 'unlock community initiative' (which presumably is already there, waiting to be set free) than simply to give resources additional to what justice would require for the benefit of people whose only claim to those resources lies in their geographical location.

RESEARCH AND POLICY

Throughout the period discussed in this book, the relationship between research and policy was a close, but often contentious and controversial, one. Consequently policies to tackle urban deprivation or the problems of the inner-city provide an important case study of the association between research, or more generally social science, and policy. The subject is one that has involved a great deal of social scientific enquiry and, more particularly, it is an area of policy where government departments have called on the advice of social scientists. Indeed, it is arguable that there have been more social scientists working in this area of policy than virtually any other over the last 15 years, but that is not to say that they have necessarily been influential.

The CDP was an action-*research* programme. The Urban Programme was evaluated by social scientists; several individual social scientists served on influential committees of enquiry, such as Milner Holland, Plowden and Seebohm, which related directly to problems of urban deprivation and also a number of social scientists within government were working in this policy area. To explore the association between research and policy further it would be useful to review how social science relates to the policy process, and we can consider this under a number of pragmatic headings.

The move towards area strategies to combat deprivation did not grow in an intellectual vacuum. Rather, it occurred at a time of growing concern about poverty and the persistence of inequality. Social science research and teaching did much to stimulate concern about deprivation. This is hardly surprising, given the traditional social science concern with questions of class, status and power. The 1960s and the 1970s were a period of unprecedented growth in the social sciences in Britain. More university departments were opened, independent research centres were created, social scientists entered the government service (the economists and statisticians establishing strong footholds, the sociologists and social administrators occupying more tentative positions), and individual social scientists became influential as advisers to government, members of committees of enquiry, pressure group activists and part-time pundits. It can be no coincidence that the growth of the social sciences and the developing interest in problems of urban deprivation occurred at much the same time.

Social scientific interest in causation, and in the association between different social problems, shifted attention towards the concept of 'deprivation'. Whereas in the 1950s the focus of attention was usually on subject areas like housing, education and poverty, this developed in the late 1960s and 1970s into a focus on deprivation, be it 'multiple', 'transmitted' or 'urban'. There was interest in the links between social problems and a reluctance to study problems in isolation. Thus those concerned, initially, with problems of educational attainment became more interested in looking at this issue in relation to questions of housing, income and class. Housing specialists started to focus on the housing market and the city, while those concerned with poverty started to consider questions of income distribution and employment markets. Not surprisingly, this general interest quickly (and perhaps rather casually) started to shift attention towards the problems of deprived *areas*. It was at this time, as Donnison has remarked, that 'social policy goes spatial' (Donnison and Soto, 1980).

The diagnosis of social ills, however, is not an apolitical process: at least, it is one that has political implications. The more comprehensive the diagnosis, the greater the likelihood that recommendations flowing from research will be radical and challenging. Analysing homelessness, for example, purely in terms of housing allocation and administrative arrangements may pose awkward questions for administrators, but an analyis that places the problems of the homeless in the context of local housing markets will pose more difficult questions for those in power. The story of the CDP is a classic illustration of this process; for what the Home Office conceived as a project concerned with several rather specific social problems, which it was hoped would be amenable to greater local co-ordination and imagination at the level of social service provision, became, as we have seen, a political hot potato when CDP teams broadened their work to analyse such matters as employment and housing markets, the structure and ownership of industry and central government's own role and interest in promoting anti-poverty programmes. The CDP, however, points to a dilemma for researchers, for while its analysis was, at one level, challenging and radical, it was easy for officials to convince their Departments and their own ministers (Labour ministers) that the work was now so 'political' that it had lost any objectivity and therefore did not deserve serious attention. CDP reports were not only political; they were were written up in the most overt political language. It was an embarrassing project for the Home Office, but in the context of that Department's overall responsibilities, and the problems facing the Labour administration of the day, it was little more than a mild irritant.

Measuring the scale, intensity and characteristics of social problems is a well understood aspect of social science, and one that is clearly of value to policy-makers. However, the relationship between researchers and policy-makers here is not an easy one. There are problems about time scale and about answering the seemingly 'simple' questions posed by administrators and ministers. These points can be illustrated with reference to the frequent demand, through the period, for a list of the 'worst' or 'most deprived' areas in the country.

This is a perfectly reasonable question for policy-makers to ask, but from the social scientist's viewpoint it is not straightforward. What is meant by 'worst'? And how are the deprivations in such areas measured? While the Census provides data on certain aspects of deprivation and is particularly strong on housing, it is less useful for certain other aspects. Even for housing, what may appear from Census data to be a well housed area, with large proportions of households possessing all the basic amenities, may in practice camouflage an area of low-quality, high-rise local authority housing, set in the very worst physical environment. Other indicators of deprivation may be seriously misleading – the numbers of children in care, for example, may tell more about the local practice of child care than about the nature of family need.

There will often be serious problems of timing. Social scientists will be able to gather better data, and therefore to produce more authoritative answers to policy-makers' questions, but it will take time. As noted in chapter 4, a Home Office request to OPCS for data on a certain issue took 18 months to produce results – not very helpful for the official who needs to present the names of six authorities to his minister next week.

But without good statistics, serious mistakes can be made. Indeed, at the time when there was most interest in multiple deprivation, there was little available evidence on the multiplicity of deprivation *within* households. Statistics that reveal an area to contain 30 per cent of households without a basic housing amenity and 30 per cent of households with an unemployed head tell us nothing about the proportion of households that both *lack* the amenity and suffer from unemployment. Yet such statistics can too easily be interpreted as evidence of multiple deprivation.

In practice, 'facts' will be just one of many influences on the decisions of government departments. The selection of areas for new deprivation programmes will often be as much influenced by, say, the quality of the chief executive, local politics, the need for a spread of areas throughout Great Britain or the need to avoid too many projects in London, as by more objective indicators of need.

Facts will also be either ignored or taken into account, depending on practical convenience. As the story of the CCP showed, the evidence about the relative *lack* of concentration of deprivation was ignored during the early phase of the project, when a small-area focus was in vogue, but was used as justification for changing the direction of CCP policy when this became necessary.

Given the broad nature of urban deprivation and the range of possible policy responses to it, it is not surprising that policy in this area has been characterized by a desire to experiment and to proceed cautiously. Thus, the CDP was developed as an action–research programme. Action on the ground was to be carefully monitored and evaluated and reported upon. This supposed a rational process from which new and better policy would emerge. Similarly, with the CCP, although the term 'experiment' was deliberately avoided, this programme was to proceed initially through a series of 'trial runs', which would be monitored before a full-scale national programme was launched. In practice, the monitoring and evaluation of urban deprivation strategies proceed differently from expectations and in a more haphazard and unscientific manner. Apart from the general difficulties of action–research in this area and the particular troubles of the CDP, there is also a time scale problem that is important. In practice, during the 1970s policy-makers anxious to develop new initiatives found that they were not able to wait for the research output from the preceding initiative. Thus, the PAR on urban deprivation was set up prior to, and was consequently not informed by, most of the CDP publications. Similarly, the CCP itself was not even off the ground before there were pressures to review and develop new policies to tackle the problems of the inner-city.

Much social scientific effort is concerned with the review of past and existing policies and analysing options for the future. Here too urban deprivation provided fertile territory for the work of researchers and social scientists. However, in this area again the relationship between researchers and policy-makers is not always an easy one. At the outset of any new policy review, when the search for new ideas and new solutions is on within Whitehall, social scientists in universities and research institutes are often courted by officials. At this stage, the comprehensive approach to questions will prove attractive. However, the relationship between policy and research is more difficult later on in the policy process. The options that are favoured for administrative, financial and political reasons may not be the ones recommended by social scientists who are influenced more by evidence of need and underlying causation. Thus, within the Home Office Urban Deprivation Unit, the concern of the Unit's social scientists with questions of employment, industrial location and the need for a joint approach to social policy in this area initially proved interesting to policy-makers, but over time became embarrassing and unhelpful. As the CCP became little more than the policy instrument to encourage greater coordination at local level, the social scientists' concern with 'structural' issues was regarded as an irritant, and, as the balance of power within the unit shifted decisively in favour of the administrators – as it was always likely to do – social scientists were pushed into less pressing aspects of the unit's work.

Research does not only inform policy through the output of thorough going and often expensive research studies. It is also influential, sometimes more influential, in less formal ways via the advice offered, or sought from, individual social scientists. Donnison has noted the impact of such individuals on social policy-making in Britain and has observed that 'many of these people – often the ones who enjoy the gritty detail – also enjoy attempting more comprehensive assessments of society and the directions in which it is heading' (Donnison and Soto, 1980). Certainly in the field of urban policy many such individuals, through their service on committees of enquiry or by the advice that they were able to offer individual policy makers, help determine the future of urban deprivation strategies. This kind of advice-giving is certainly open to risk. Indeed, it has been suggested that the advocacy of the area approach involved social scientists in 'overselling the knowledge base'. And with reference to the Plowden Committee and its recommendations in favour of Education Priority Areas, it has been said that the Committee was unsure about the focus of its study and at times spoke of deprived children, deprived schools and deprived areas, without spelling out the different significance for policy strategy.

While some individual academics were prepared to advise policy-makers on the future direction of policy, others were more content to sit back and offer critical appraisals of past policy. Indeed, many social scientists during this period seemed better able, and possibly more willing to provide critical commentaries on the course of, for example, the CDP experiment, than actively to suggest the lessons of past policy failures and hence the future direction of policy. This far from constructive contribution from many social scientists was partly the product of the secretive nature of decision-making in Whitehall in this area of policy, as in so many others. Apart from a few eminent social scientists, and one or two favoured research institutes, most social scientists with an interest in this area were not aware of the policy developments taking place and thus, unwittingly, were often in the position of producing critical appraisals that were several years behind the policy action. This was certainly often the view of social scientists within Whitehall, who found their colleagues unaware of current concerns within government and the important questions calling out for good debate. The lack of openness in central government decision–making is at the root of this problem. Thus, for example, between 1974 and 1977 there were three internal reviews of urban deprivation policy: none of them was published and only one was ever publicly announced. It is hardly surprising, in this closed context, that outside academics were seldom able to make an impact on Whitehall decision-making, or that the advice they offered often seemed irrelevant to the issues under discussion within Whitehall.

RACE

The issue of race has been a counterpoint to the various themes running through the different programmes described in these pages. It is, however, a striking fact that, although racial problems were 'present at the creation' of many of the programmes, they were rarely confronted directly or explicitly. Despite the initial intention to address the issue in the course of implementing the programmes, it has in each case rapidly receded to a position of secondary importance or in some instances, has disappeared altogether from view. This has been true even with the Urban Programme and inner-cities policy, where the focus on race was quite distinct. How can this be explained?

There are three possible lines of explanation. The first is simply that the British administrative and legal systems are inherently resistant to dealing explicitly with race in any circumstances. The ethos of 'colour blindness' has become so firmly established that it is now second nature to judges and administrators to claim that law and policy make no distinctions between equal citizens; when distinctions are admitted, they are cloaked by the use of some such (presumed) neutral term as 'inner-city' inhabitants. The principle of compensation for disadvantage on a territorial basis became quite widely accepted during the currency of the special programmes examined in this book; primacy for ethnic minorities as such has not, and Young and Connelly's recent research shows how tenacious resistance still is, in social services departments in particular (1981).

Administrative tradition is one possible explanation: another, more cynical, one is political advantage. Politicians of both major parties are wary of taking measures that will identify them with policies that appear to be favouring minorities at the expense of the majority, especially at times when resources are scarce. The rhetoric of colour-blindness can be called into play to legitimize this stance, but it is ultimately based on straightforward calculations of electoral advantage (see the Crossman Diaries for a particularly vivid expose of the process at work: Crossman, 1977). One result of this reluctance is that there are no effective spokesmen for the interests of minorities at the point of decision-taking on resource allocation.

The third type of explanation concerns the administrative structure within which decisions about race relations policies have been made – both generally and in the case of the programmes discussed here. The Home Office, who had the primary responsibility for such matters, was unwilling to see an ethnic emphasis in the programmes. Despite the Department's coordinating role in the Urban Programme, the CDP and the CCP, there was an apparent reluctance to see a more comprehensive attack upon the problems of racial disadvantage. As the Home Office relinquished its position to the DOE in the late 1970s, it became only marginal to the setting of priorities. The opportunity to use its involvement with the inner-city Partnerships to introduce race relations on to the agenda, in a more systematic way, was never taken up. This was particularly evident in Lambeth, where (despite having the oldest established West Indian settlement) it was simply left to the borough's energetic race relations unit to put forward issues for discussion and to formulate policy.

One of the most significant developments has been that the responsibility for policies on race has been widely dispersed with the creation, from the 1960s onwards, of various QUANGOS such as the Race Relations Board, the Community Relations Commission, the National Committee for Commonwealth Immigrants and the Commission for Racial Equality. Although some impact has been made on 'petty' discrimination, the policy development role has never been effective owing largely to the fact that the agencies are cut off from the centres of power and policy-making. Only at rare intervals (for example, Roy Jenkins in the late 1960s and briefly in the mid-1970s) have senior ministers concerned themselves with the issue for any length of time. Without such support and sponsorship, the chances of any QUANGOS making an impact in areas such as inner-city programmes have been severely limited. Certainly, the attempts of the Commission for Racial Equality to become involved in such policy areas have led nowhere.

On the other hand, it has been argued that the lack of an explicit 'ethnic' dimension in inner-city policy is not, necessarily, disadvantageous. David Kirp, for example, suggests that it is only when race is not salient that there is any real prospect of achieving significant progress. Without pressure from the public arena, administrators would be free to develop policies that redistribute resources, within reasonable limits, without the need to mount expensive, controversial and probably self-defeating demonstration projects. While there may be a point here, the argument generally has its limitations. It ignores the importance, both for majority and minority groups, of being seen to make progress. In particular, it overlooks the role of ethnic minority organizations who depend upon visible outcomes in order to retain their constituency. This aspect was clearly illustrated by experiences in Lambeth.

Can it be argued that some progress has in fact been made by 'stealth' in the course of the various programmes, despite the failure to deal with racial issues directly? The question cannot be answered with any degree of precision because of the lack of systematic records against which improvements could be measured. However, the evidence from earlier chapters indicates that progress has been, at best, patchy. The selection of areas has benefited minorities to some degree – in a semi-colour-blind way – but there have been few, if any, systematic attempts to target funds within any particular local programme towards minorities; the nearest example is the Lambeth case. The fact that not one of the politicians dealing with resource allocation, at national or local level, was black may be significant here. It is certainly a contrast with the

American situation, where the influence of the voting public has ensured that the interests of blacks are taken into account when resources are distributed.

The position of ethnic minorities in British society cannot be said to have improved noticeably as a result of the programmes discussed here. While their problems persist, there seems to be no greater commitment to resolving them in the 1980s than there was in the 1960s when some of these programmes began. The issues of racial disadvantage and discrimination continue to bubble beneath the surface of political life, and only periodically, as in the riots of 1981, do they command public attention. Lord Scarman's much misunderstood plea for 'positive' discrimination' (actually a plea for the implementation of policies enshrined in the 1976 Race Relations Act) could lead to positive action, but is unlikely to go far towards a full resolution of the problems.

PROGRESS OR CHANGE?

Finally, what can we say about 14 years of inner-city policies? What have we learned about the inner-city problem over this period? Has there been a linear progression of knowledge or a change of orthodoxies? Do we have a better and more accurate diagnosis of the inner-city problem today than we did in 1967, and do we have a clearer vision of what success would look like? As far as policy is concerned, what experience have we gained: do we now know better what must be done to alleviate the problems of inner areas? In taking stock of the 14 years of inner-city policies, these are the questions to which we must seek an answer.

We have characterized (perhaps caricatured) the shift in conception of the inner-city problem from one of pathology to one of structure, but perhaps this is an oversimplification. The problems of the elderly, dependent and handicapped do not disappear simply by refocusing on economic infrastructure. What we call the' inner-city problem is multi-factorial and multi-faceted. It consists (whether as cause, condition or manifestation) of poor housing and environment, poor educational achievement, poverty, high rates of health morbidity (and mortality), delinquency, illiteracy and crime, large numbers of one-parent and large families (and of the handicapped, inadequate, and the unskilled), high rates of unemployment, few job opportunities, increasing job losses and low economic investment. We have seen how urban deprivation policies were born not out of a primary concern with any of these, but in response to the immigration and race relations issue. This was overlaid for presentational purposes (in the Urban Programme) by a diagnosis of deprivation that was little more than an uncoordinated reiteration of the most obvious features of inner-city areas. No attempt to incorporate an analysis of the causes of these manifestations was made, but for the early years of urban deprivation policies, at least, there was an implicit assumption that the problem was both residual and relatively geographically concentrated. What began to happen with the CDP (and to a lesser extent the CCP) – gaining currency with the Inner Areas Studies, acquiring legitimacy with the 1977 White Paper and achieving the status of orthodoxy with the post 1977 initiatives – was an emphasis on *different* components of the inner-city problem: namely, job loss, decaying economic infrastructure, and lack of investment in the inner cities. While, morally, this seems a more acceptable position (at least we no longer 'blame' the victims), is it a more accurate diagnosis? It can be argued that a structural analysis concentrates on the *causes* of the inner-city problem rather than on its manifestations, and to this extent it must be preferred. This argument is less than convincing, however, and so far as it underpins present initiatives *to the exclusion of other arguments* it may be damaging. Decaying economic infrastructure (and all that that entails) cannot be said to be the direct cause of high rates of health and social morbidities, of high proportions of large and one-parent families, the handicapped, the inadequate, of low educational achievement or (directly at least) of poor housing and poor environments. What we have achieved since 1976 is a *different* analysis rather than necessarily a better one; our conceptions of the inner-city problem have changed rather than progressed, and perhaps we have simply exchanged one orthodoxy for another.

What, then, are the policy implications of this? Present

policies such as Partnership and Programme arrangements, designations under the Inner Urban Areas Act 1978, the Urban Development Corporations and Enterprise Zones are primarily directed at increasing economic investment in the inner cities – attracting industry and commerce back and thereby increasing the number of jobs there. What might this achieve if, as seems unlikely, it is successful? Will the jobs so created go to the ranks of inner-city unemployed (including the unskilled, the young and the black)? It seems far from certain that they will, in the absence of measures specifically to ensure it. Again, inner-city economic regeneration, especially if left primarily to private entrepreneurs, as is the case at present, is not in itself a redistributive mechanism. Such a strategy alone will not help the poor, the handicapped, the one-parent families and all the other disadvantaged residents of the inner-city. It would seem unduly optimistic to expect the market, even with the help of the various forms of incentive offered by current policies, to operate in the inner cities in favour of those groups that in society as a whole are its main victims. Much, of course, will depend on the precise configuration of the inner-area programmes assembled by the Partnership and the Programme authorities and the extent to which the private sector is relied upon to effect economic regeneration: but the close compatibility of the post-1976 diagnosis with the confidence of the Conservative government in the ability of the private sector to effect change suggests that this sector will indeed be charged with the dominant role.

It has to be said, therefore, that the post-1977 policies and the conceptions of the problem on which they are founded remain, like the policies and conceptions that preceded them, partial formulations. We are still attacking only part of the problem – though a different part. If the Urban Programme was (and is) concerned with assisting the deprived to the exclusion of a concern for more fundamental economic problems, the major thrust of the post–1977 initiatives is in danger of leaving them to their fate. So long as one set of policy initiatives is (in part at least) a reaction against preceding initiatives, the possibility of a policy response as multi-faceted as the problems it seeks to tackle remains remote.

The conclusions of this book are generally pessimistic.

Although we have greatly added to our store of knowledge in the last 14 years, about urban policy-making and practice, we are no nearer to a political resolution of the problems we have outlined. It is clear, from all the research reports at our disposal, that the answer to our urban problems required the investment of huge resources. There are no cheap solutions. It is equally clear that urban poverty in all its aspects (not least the racial element) is low on the list of priorities in central government. There are a number of possible outcomes. One is what S.M. Miller describes as 're-inventing the broken wheel'. In other words, we can go on devising more of the same kind of piecemeal programmes to deal with parts of the problem. Another would be to put muscle into the notion of a genuinely coordinated and 'total approach' to the cities. A third would be to reject the notion of spatial programmes in favour of a 'people-based' approach. Yet another would be to do nothing new and to settle for short-term 'crisis intervention' as and when the need arises. Whichever option is chosen, there can be no excuse for an uninformed decision. Fourteen years of research has provided a wealth of data which can describe, explain and prescribe. They can provide no perfect answers but, used selectively, they would overcome the tendency to 'muddle through' that is so characteristic of British urban policy-making. Without a more rational and positive approach, it seems only a question of waiting for the explosion of another urban time-bomb such as those we have seen in Brixton, Moss Side and Toxteth.

Notes

Chapter 3   The Urban Programme

1 Separate arrangements have always existed for Scotland.
2 The London Docklands ceased to be a Partnership area when granted Urban Development Corporation status in 1981.
3 The account that follows is based largely on the fuller account given in Edwards and Batley (1978). The reader wishing for the details necessarily left out of the present account is referred to chs 2, 3 and 5 of that book.
4 'The basic aim of the Urban Programme is to alleviate deprivation in local areas of acute social need' (Home Office, 1972).
5 On the Urban Programme especially, see Edwards and Batley (1978, ch.2). The 'rediscovery of poverty' and the awakening of concern over the possible failure of the 'Beveridge ideals' are in some measure attributable to the following works: Abel-Smith and Townsend (1965); Lynes (1963); Lambert (1963); Central Advisory Committee for Education (1959, 1963). In the field of housing the Report of the Committee on Housing in Greater London (Milner Holland, Report, 1965) was influential in drawing attention to poor housing conditions and being one of the first calls for *intra-city* priority area action. For an account of American programmes, see Higgins, (1978) and Hambleton (1978, ch. 6).
6 'Restrictive immigration rules, and widespread public knowledge that these rules are restrictive, are a necessary condition for the general acceptance of the minority communities. . . .' (leader in *The Times*, 10 July 1981, on the riots in Brixton, Toxteth and elsewhere.
7 This information is based on conversations held with senior

administrators during the course of research on the Urban Programme betwen 1972 and 1975.

8 It is worth noting in this context however that, during the period of inner-city riots on 4 – 12 July 1981, governmental response in the media and in the House of Commons came entirely from the Home Office (with some interjections from the Secretary of State for Employment). The DOE, which carries responsibility for inner-city policies, was entirely silent.

9 The committee referred to was to run parallel with and be serviced by the working party.

10 The Urban Programme was of course widely known among local authorities and voluntary organizations, but it was also widely cited in the press in the context of inner-city deprivation.

11 These were established as a result of the recommendations of the Plowden Report (Central Advisory Committee for Education, 1968).

12 These operated largely for slum clearance purposes.

13 This figure is the sum of all approval costs under circulars 1–17.

14 Two of these exist at present, one each for Merseyside and London Docklands.

15 A rate of 75 per cent was decided on. The local authority associations argued (unrealistically) for a 100 per cent grant, the Treasury for a 50 per cent grant and the Home Office for 75 per cent. The issue was decided at ministerial level.

16 It is also specifically ruled out in the 1977 White Paper DOE, 1977, para. 14).

17 This is reflected in the increase in employment – relevant projects funded by the programme in recent years; see pp. 82–85.

18 Though represented on the Working Party, the Department of Employment and Productivity never received its own block of UP funds for allocation.

19 Though initially – as explained above – monies for the programme came from departmental savings, from 1971 the programme became a first call on the rate support grant pool.

20 The allocation for 1980/81 (at 1980/81 out-turn prices) was:

	£ million
Partnerships	110.8
Programme authorities	42.0
Traditional Urban Programme	33.6
Industrial Projects under IUA Act 1978	5.6
Other items	13.8
	205.8

Source: DOE, 1981b

21 This account draws on information given during conversations with the Under Secretary, Assistant Secretary and Principal in the Inner Cities Directorate at the DOE in June 1981.

22 The degree of support (although not unmixed with criticism) from local authorities and voluntary agencies has been documented in Edwards and Batley (1978; see especially ch. 7).

23 It should be added that this view is not supported by officials currently (1981) responsible for the programme.

24 The Lewisham Law Centre was cited as an example of a case of a minister intervening with the local authority on the grounds that the Centre was acting overtly as a political pressure group.

25 Since the programme's inception, 5,510 projects have been approved. Of these, 600 were holiday projects (one-off events). Some other projects may have ended with time-expiry of funds.

26 The 25 categories were devised during the first evaluation of the programme and have been kept to enable recent data to be combined with those for earlier phases. Recent changes in the types of project funded would suggest a slightly different classification if beginning anew.

27 These figures include holiday projects, which accounts for the slight differences to the figures in table 2.

28 That this was the predominant view of the programme among local authorities also was confirmed by the two evaluations of it (Edwards and Batley, 1978. pp. 180–2; and DOE, 1980b para. 3, 16).

29 Published as Edwards and Batley (1978) a shortened and (for publication) censored version of a longer report submitted to the Home Office in 1976.

30 This is a judgement based on the brief summary under the heading 'The Review' in para. 2 of Urban Programme Circular no. 21 (DOE, 1980a). The results of the review were also influential in the decision in 1980 to keep the Programme going, but it is not possible to say to what extent this decision was *determined* by the results of the review and to what extent by other considerations.

31 It should be noted that the review does not claim that this was a thorough assessment, and the author of it emphasizes its limitations.

32 This is not to say that individual projects are not evaluable; See Edwards and Batley, 1974.

33 In the twenty-first circular, the description is transferred to the application form, presumably in the interests of brevity.

34 A rhetorical flourish this; what it would entail in practice is difficult to say.

35 At the same time, the circular insists that the 'main thrust of the Government's attack on unemployment among young people is the Youth Opportunities Programme'.

36 The gap that exists, however, between the sort of incentives that such projects (and other parts of inner-city policy) provide and the considerations most crucial to potentially mobile industry is particularly well demonstrated in an excellent article by D. Cadman (1979).

37 For brevity, the condensed project classification is used here: see table 2, Note B.

Chapter 4   *The Lost Years*

1 Others have pointed to the police and general 'law and order' responsibilities of the Home Office as being important. In terms of 'social control' theories this may make sense, but I have not found this to be relevant in practice.

2 The author of this chapter was Social Policy Analyst at the Unit between 1974 and 1977.

3 While later critics of the CCP were to attack the Programme as being firmly rooted within a 'social pathology' model, this was never a justifiable criticism and said more about the out-of-date nature of the critics' analysis than about the state of thinking within Whitehall.

4 Given the past history of area approaches, any new initiative was likely to be greeted with such a cynical response. Urban Deprivation Unit staff hoped these events would prove such cynicism groundless – they didn't.

5 The Urban Deprivation Unit recruited a social scientist with a statistical background to work specifically on these issues. During his first weeks he requested, from the OPCS runs of data on multiple deprivation within enumeration districts. About two years later, in the weeks before he left the Home Office, the first results arrived!

6 There was Treasury opposition, in July, to current CCP thinking. Treasury officials advised the Home Office that Treasury ministers would be advised 'absolutely against' public statements that had implications for public spending. The Treasury advocated 'grasping the nettle', i.e., abandoning the CCP.

7 Eventually CCPS – in practice simply coordinating exercises – were attempted in two English authorities (Gateshead and Bradford) and in Motherwell. They made little impression.

Chapter 5   Peter Shore and Inner-City Policy

1 The 1982–83 allocations, announced after this chapter was completed, do preserve the principle of Partnership,' priority, but in a much reduced general allocation.
2 The inclusion of Liverpool in this list is perhaps debatable.

References

Abel-Smith, B. and Townsend, P. (1965), *The Poor and the Poorest*, Bell, London.

Banting, K. (1979), *Poverty, Politics and Policy*, Macmillan, London.

Barnes, J. (1974), 'A solution to whose problem?', in Howard Glennerster and Stephen Hatch (eds), *Positive Discrimination and Inequality*, Fabian Research Series no. 314, Fabian Society, London

Benn, S. and Peters, R. (1959), *Social Principles and the Democratic State*, Allen and Unwin, London.

Bridges, Lee (1975) 'The Ministry of Internal Security: British urban social policy, 1968–74', *Race and Class*, xvi, 4.

Brown, Muriel and Baldwin, Sally (1978), *The Yearbook of Social Policy in Britain, 1977*, Routledge & Kegan Paul, London.

Burney, E. (1967), *Housing on Trial*, Oxford University Press.

Cadman, D. (1979), 'Private capital and the inner city', *Estates Gazette*, vol. 249, no. 5927, 31 March.

Callaghan, J. (1968), Statement on the Urban Programme, *Hansard*, vol. 769, 22 July.

Castle, Barbara (1980), *The Castle Diaries*, Weidenfeld & Nicolson, London.

CDP (1974), *Inter-Project Report, 1973*, Home Office, London.

CDP (1975), *The Poverty of the Improvement Programme*, Information and Intelligence Unit, London.

CDP (1976a), *Whatever happened to Council Housing?*, Information and Intelligence Unit, London.

CDP (1976b), *Profits against Houses*, Information and Intelligence Unit, London.

CIS/CDP (1975), *Cutting the Welfare State (Who Profits?)*, Counter Information Services and CDP Information Unit, London.

CDP (1977a), *The Costs of Industrial Change*, Home Office, London.

CDP (1977b), *Gilding the Ghetto; the State and the Poverty Experiments*, Home Office, London.

Central Advisory Committee for Education (1959), *Fifteen to Eighteen* (Crowther Report), HMSO, London.

Central Advisory Committee for Education (1963), *Half our Future* (Newsom Report), HMSO, London.

Central Advisory Committee for Education (1968), *Children and their Primary Schools* (Plowden Report), HMSO, London.

Cockburn, C. (1978), *The Local State*, Pluto Press, London.

Cohen, M., Nagel, T. and Scanlon, T. (eds) (1977), *Equality and Preferential Treatment*, Princeton University Press.

Corkey, D. and Craig, G. (1978), 'CDP – community work or class politics?', in P. Curno (ed.), *Political Issues and Community Work*, Routledge & Kegan Paul, London.

Crossman, R. (1977), *The Diaries of a Cabinet Minister*, vol. 3, Hamish Hamilton, London.

Daniel, W. (1968), *Racial Discrimination in England*, Penguin, Harmondsworth.

Deakin, N. (1974), 'On some perils of limitation', in Richard Rose (ed.) *Lessons from America*, Macmillan, London.

DOE (1976) (Department of the Environment), Press release no. 835, 17 September.

DOE (1977a), *Unequal City, Final Report of the Birmingham Inner Area Study*, DOE, London.

DOE (1977b), *Inner London: Policies for Dispersal and Balance, Final Report of the Lambeth Inner Area Study*, DOE, London.

DOE (1977c), *Change and Decay. Final Report of the Liverpool Inner Area Study*, DOE, London.

DOE (1977d), *Inner Area Studies: Summaries of Consultants' Final Reports*, DOE, London.

DOE (1977e), *Policy for the Inner Cities*, Cmnd, 6845, HMSO, London.

DOE (1977f), Urban Programme Circular, no. 17.

DOE (1977g), Press release no. 63, 9 February.

DOE (1978a), Press release no. 520, 26 August.

DOE (1978b) Urban Programme Circular, no. 18.

DOE (1979), Urban Programme Circular, no. 20.

DOE (1980a), Urban Programme Circular, no. 21.

DOE (1980b), 'Review of the traditional urban programme consultative document', Inner Cities Directorate, mimeo.

DOE (1981a) 'Review of Inner Cities Policy', press notice no. 59, 9 February.

DOE (1981b), 'Factual background document to present inner-city policy and Urban Programme', Inner Cities Directorate, mimeo.

Donnison, D. (1982), *The Politics of Poverty*, Martin Robertson, Oxford.

Donnison, D. and Soto, P. (1980), *The Good City*, Heinemann, London.

Edwards, J. and Batley, R. (1974), 'The Urban Programme: a report on some programme-funded projects', *British Journal of Social Work*, vol. 4, no. 3.

Edwards, J. and Batley, R. (1978), *The Politics of Positive Discrimination*, Tavistock, London.

Feinberg, J. (1973), *Social Philosophy*, Prentice-Hall, Englewood Clifts, NJ.

Freeson, Reg (1974), 'Housing Centre Trust', speech, 4 July.

Goldman, A. (1979), *Justice and Reverse Discrimination*, Princeton University Press.

Greve, J. (1973), 'The British Community Development Project: some interim comments', *Community Development Journal*, vol. 8, no. 3.

Hall, P. (1976), *Reforming the Welfare*, Heinemann, London.

Hall, P. (1977), 'The inner cities dilemma', *New Society*, vol. 39 no. 748, 3 February.

Hall, P. Land, H. Parker, R. and Webb, A. (1975), *Change, Choice and Conflict in Social Policy*, Heinemann, London.

Hambleton, R. (1978), *Policy, Planning and Local Government*, Hutchinson, London.

Hambleton, R. (1981), 'Implementing inner-city policy', *Policy and Politics*, vol. 9, no. 1.

Hansard (1977), Debate on urban affairs, vol. 923, 14 January.

Harvey, D. (1973), *Social Justice and the City*, Edward Arnold, London.

Hatch, S. Fox, E. and Legg, C. (1977), *Research and Reform: Southwark CDP, 1969-72*, Home Office, London.

Heclo, H. and Widavsky, A. (1974), *The Private Government of Public Money*, Macmillan, London.

Heseltine, M. (1981), Statement on Inner City Policy, *Hansard* (weekly), no. 1195, 9 February.

Higgins, J. (1978), *The Poverty Business: Britain and America*, Basil Blackwell, Oxford.

Higgins, J. (1980), 'The unfulfilled promise of policy research', *Social Policy and Administration*, vol. 14, no. 3.

HMSO (1975), *A Joint Framework for Social Policies* HMSO, London.

HMSO (1977), Department of the Environment, *Inner Area Studies; Liverpool, Birmingham and Lambeth: Summaries of Consultants' Final Reports*, HMSO, London.

Holtermann, S.B. (1975a), 'Areas of urban deprivation in Great Britain', *Social Trends*, HMSO, London.

Holtermann, S. (1975b), 'Census indicators of urban deprivation', Working Note no. 6, DOE, ECUR Division.

Home Office (1968a), Draft paper on the Urban Programme.

Home Office (1968b), Working party on immigration and community relations, Minutes, May 1968.

Home Office (1968c), Urban Programme Circular, no. 1.

Home Office (1969), 'Experiments in social policy and their evaluation', unpublished report of an Anglo-American conference, Ditchley Park, Oxon, 29–31 October.

Home Office (1972), Urban Programme Circular, no. 7.

Home Office (1976), Urban Programme Circular, no. 16.

Jenkins, Roy (1972), *What Matters Now*, Fontana, London.

King, T. (1980), Written Answer on Traditional Urban Programme, *Hansard*, vol. 981, no. 151, 2 April.

Kirp, D. (1979) *Doing Good by Doing Little*, University of California Press, Berkeley.

Lambert, R. (1963), *Nutrition in Britain, 1950–60*, Occasional Papers in Social Administration, Codicote Press, Welwyn Garden City.

Lawless, P. (1979), *Urban Deprivation and Government Initiative*, Faber & Faber, London.

Lawless, P. (1981), *Britain's Inner Cities: Problems and Policies*, Harper & Row, London.

Lees, R. and Smith, G. (1975), *Action-research in Community Development*, Routledge & Kegan Paul, London.

Loney, M. (1981), 'The British Community Development Projects: questioning the state, *Community Development Journal*, vol. 16, no. 1.

Lynes, A. (1963), *National Assistance and National Prosperity*, Occasional Papers in Social Administration, Codicote Press, Welwyn Garden City.

McKay, D. and Cox, A. (1979), *The Politics of Urban Change*, Croom Helm, London.

Mayo, M. (1975), 'The history and early development of CDP', in Lees and Smith (1975).

Miller, S.M. (1973), 'The case for positive discrimination', *Social Policy*, vol. 4, no. 3.

Milner Holland Report (1965), *Report of the Committee on Housing in Greater London*, Cmnd, 2605, HMSO, London.

Nabarro, R. (1980), 'Inner-city partnerships', *Town Planning Review*, vol. 51, no. 1

Pahl, R. (1970), *Whose City?*, Penguin, Harmondsworth.

Rex, J. and Moore, R. (1967), *Race, Community and Conflict*, Oxford, University Press

Righter, R. (1977), *Save our Cities*, Gulbenkian Trust, London.

Scarman Report (1981), *The Brixton Disorders, 10–12 April, 1981*, Cmnd, 8427. HMSO, London.

Seebohm Report (1969), *Committee on Local Authority and Allied Personal Social Services*, Cmnd 3703, HMSO, London.

Shore, P. (1976), Speech on inner-city policy, in *Estates Gazette*, vol. 239, 23 September.

Shore, P. (1977a), Speech on inner-city policy, in *Estates Gazette, vol. 241, 1 February*.

Shore, P. (1977b), Policy statement on inner cities, Hansard, vol. 929, April.

Shore, P. (1980), 'Urban decay: its symptoms and remedies', Third Thomas Cubitt Lecture, January 1980, mimeo.

Specht, H. (1976), *The Community Development Project: National and Local Strategies for Improving the Delivery of Services*, National Institute of Social Work, London.

The Times (1981), Leader article on riots, 10 July 1981.

Wicks, Malcolm (1978), 'Social policy for the inner cities', in Brown and Baldwin (1978).

Young, Ken and Connelly, Naomi (1981), *Policy and Practice in the Multi-racial City*, Policy Studies Institute Report, no. 598, November.

Index